Walter Roy Sharp

WIGAN ROAD
DIARIES OF A VALUATION SURVEYOR

AUSTIN MACAULEY PUBLISHERS
LONDON · CAMBRIDGE · NEW YORK · SHARJAH

Copyright © Walter Roy Sharp 2025

The right of **Walter Roy Sharp** to be identified as author of this work has been asserted by the author in accordance with sections 77 and 78 of the Copyright, Designs and Patents Act 1988.

All rights reserved. No part of this publication may be reproduced, stored in a retrieval system, or transmitted in any form or by any means, electronic, mechanical, photocopying, recording, or otherwise, without the prior permission of the publishers.

Any person who commits any unauthorised act in relation to this publication may be liable to criminal prosecution and civil claims for damages.

A CIP catalogue record for this title is available from the British Library.

ISBN 9781035821150 (Paperback)
ISBN 9781035821174 (ePub e-book)

www.austinmacauley.com

First Published 2025
Austin Macauley Publishers Ltd®
1 Canada Square
Canary Wharf
London
E14 5AA

For my perfect wife, Kate Sharp.

Let's raise our hats to John Whittaker.

Saxon White Kessinger – *The Indispensable Man*

Charles Moore – *The Authorised Biography of Margaret Thatcher*

Gerry and Gill Hamilton for photographs and information.

Christina Mercer, the landlady of the Albion.

Ex. Colleagues—Alisdair McNicol, Paul Dowsett, Neil Clarke and John Wood for photographs and memory support.

Google has been used in the book for dates and facts.

Table of Contents

Synopsis	10
Growing up in Wigan Road	11
Bomb Disposal Team	20
After the War	24
The 1960s	29
Manchester	43
Las Vegas of the North	54
Coal	56
Life as a Local Government Officer	62
Terminal Cancer	66
Peterborough Development Corporation	72
My Job at Peterborough	75
Property Development Service	87
Cheshire County Council	97
My Local	116
Group Development Manager CWS	119

Joint Development Companies	**127**
The End Game at CWS	**142**
Co-op Retailing Takes Over	**145**
Redundancy	**147**
Ellesmere Port and Neston Borough Council	**150**
ACES	**163**
Buy to Let	**167**
Days in the Sun	**169**
Retirement	**172**
Appendix	**178**

Synopsis

This book is about a valuation surveyor who started his working life in Manchester working for Richard Hoyle & Company, in St Ann's Square. Hoyles had been established by the Cotton Barons to deal with the insurance industry. The barons were not receiving good settlements after fire damage. Hoyles was taken over by Edward Ruston Son and Kenyon in 1962.

After 9 years with ERS&K, he moved into public service with Salford City Council, Peterborough Development Corporation, Cheshire County Council and Ellesmere Port & Neston Borough Council. He also worked for the Cooperative movement twice. The first time advising retail societies and the second time as a group manager responsible for property development and joint property development companies nationally.

Walter was responsible for the purchase of the Nene Valley Railway, the land for the Orton Township in Peterborough and many other major projects in England, Scotland and Northern Ireland.

He was a property adviser to one of the north's largest superannuation funds for 11 years and played amateur rugby league and rugby union for Tyldesley.

He became an expert in using local authorities as a catalyst to maximise their financial return from property.

Growing up in Wigan Road

I am writing my autobiography having recently celebrated my 80th birthday. My intention is to factually record my life experience, which will conclude that, like it or loathe it, who I am was forged in Wigan Road, Leigh. I was born in Leigh, on the 17 February 1943, in Firs Maternity Hospital.

Leigh was then a town with a population of approximately 45,000. My mother was Marinda (Renee) Sharp, née Hall. My father was Walter Sharp, who had been killed at El-Alamein in October 1942, Sapper No 2126376, royal engineers. Killed clearing Erwin Rommel's land mines on the 22 or 23 October, before the main battle commenced.

Leigh was then a town at the epicentre of the Lancashire cotton and coal belt, in the midst of the neighbouring towns of Wigan, Warrington, Bolton and St Helens. The house I lived in with my widowed mother, until I left Leigh 28 years later, was 12 Hulme Road, off Wigan Road, and next door but two to Wigan Road working men's club.

West Leigh, one of the working-class sides of the town, virtually offered only employment in coal mines and cotton mills. I could walk from 12 Hulme Road and within 30-minutes to Bickershaw Colliery, Parsonage Colliery, West Leigh Colliery, Tunnicliffe Weaving Sheds and Hayes 7 storey Cotton Mill.

BICKERSHAW COLLIERY

Bickershaw Colliery, photo taken the week after it closed.

Submitted by Arthur Culshaw.

A mining landscape which has now completely vanished. Pithead gear at Bickershaw Colliery which was closed in 1992, the last mine in the Leigh district.

Bickershaw Colliery

J. & J. HAYES, L^{TD}

Number of Mule Spindles - 200,888
Number of Ring Spindles - 8,000

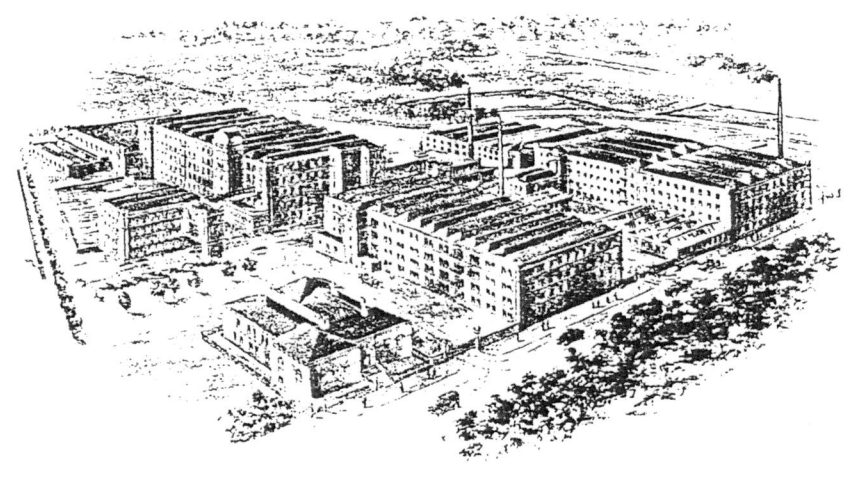

VIEW OF VICTORIA MILLS, LEIGH, LANCASHIRE

COUNTS OF YARN

36's to 54's Pin Cop
50's to 60's Bastard Cop
36's to 80's Doubling Weft
36's to 80's Twist Cop

SUPER CARDED
EGYPTIAN

BEAMS and CHEESES

VICTORIA MILLS, LEIGH
LANCASHIRE

In those days, Leigh people were, on the whole, fiercely tribal. They would be unlikely to consider any point of view but their own. Sometimes introducing themselves to opponents in rugby, football or fishing matches with the mantra, reflecting their character, "I am from Leigh; what are you going to do about it?"

Nevertheless, they had a determined and resourceful nature, but also very caring for others, when there was a need to be so. They would collectively support a deserving project e.g. building with their own resources the town's rugby league ground, Hilton Park. Those traits manifested themselves in politics. The town had always voted Labour since the Labour party had been formed.

Although there was always the unanswered question, "What had Labour ever done for Leigh?"

This was the case until the General Election of 2019 when Leigh voted Conservative. Andy Burnham, now the Mayor of Manchester, had been the Labour MP for Leigh. He is a Scouser (nothing wrong with being a Scouser) but claiming to be a local lad, I thought, went against the grain. He is now, however, doing a pretty good job as Mayor of Manchester.

Looking back at my life in Leigh, growing up in Wigan Road, my strongest memory is the strength of the local pride. It is difficult to know where this pride came from. I have never experienced it anywhere else. I could expect it in Chester, but no. My view is that it came from the two local industries of Cotton and Coal. Two industries that passed their skills to the next generation. Today Leigh is no longer a cotton and coal town, so sometimes I wonder if the town's culture has changed. It must have changed, to some degree, or it would never have voted Conservative.

My mother had no income, except for a war widow's pension. She did have a determined and proud disposition and was very ambitious for her only son, who was not going to suffer from the lack of a father. My mother never set a foot in Wigan Road working men's club, only two doors away. I was brought up attending St Peter's Church of England School. Mother and I went to church every Sunday morning, and I went to Sunday school in the afternoon.

The most significant event in my early childhood was the death of my grandad Hall in 1950. He had been a coalface worker in one of the Wigan pits. In his later working life, he had emigrated to Nova Scotia, with the intention of taking his wife and five daughters there. My grandad had found work in an open cast coalmine in Canada. Unfortunately, he broke his collarbone soon after he arrived and had to return.

My grandad, Bill Hall, is the tall man in the centre, front row.

My grandad, Bill Hall, is the tall man in the centre, front row. He then became a police officer! My mother was very proud of the photograph of the police team in Abram—he is first on the left.

My grandad died after a long struggle with lung cancer, caused by silicosis. My Nana and Grandad lived at 28 Lily Lane, Bamfurlong, located between Wigan and Abram, not far from Ashton-in-Makerfield. My mother took his death in a bad way and it increased the tears, she always shed, in church on Sunday mornings. I can remember the gathering of all the Hall family at their Bamfurlong house and remember being picked up to kiss my grandad in his coffin.

I attended St Peter's Primary School, which was located, about a 15-minute walk away from my home, through Firs Park. This was a relatively safe journey to school each day and uneventful, except when a so-called friend of mine, with a small group of his friends had decided that I should fight him. I didn't panic and hit him on the nose and he started to cry.

I cannot remember much from my infant school days, except that one day my mother had heard something on the news and thought we would be asked a question in the morning assembly about it. She was correct and the Headmistress duly asked the question, so I put my hand up and in front of the whole school, answered the question. I cannot remember what the question was about, but I have never been shy about asking difficult or embarrassing questions.

In Leigh, most of the work force had reserved occupations in the war years, being employed in cotton or coal, considered to be essential for the war effort. Therefore, the large families, that were the norm before the war, continued. This led to large class sizes in towns where the majority were not involved in the war effort. This was certainly the case at St Peter's Junior School.

The children when moving up from the infant school to the

primary school, were split into two, using the alphabet. Therefore, being called Sharp, I ended up being in a class of 56, in stream B. There was no other way of dealing with the numbers.

I remember the first day. I was in the desk in the second row from the front of the class. The girl in front of me turned round, with a smile on her face, and made a gesture that I thought was crude. I remember this because I was flummoxed. Was it a sign of hostility or friendship?

The next day I moved to the back row of the class, where I remained for the rest of the time at St Peter's School. It was noisy and nobody seemed to be in control. I felt under stress in the classroom. I constantly daydreamed and released my frustration in the break times.

I quickly learned, that if you did not put your hand up, you were never asked any questions!

At the age of nine, a friend of my mother came to stay for health treatment in Astley and stayed for several weeks. This friend pointed out that I was very backward in my learning, for my age and should by now be more advanced in English and Maths.

My courageous and resourceful mother then embarked on a plan to provide me with a decent education, that was, she thought, unavailable in the state system in Leigh, at that time.

Growing up in Leigh was a challenge in many ways. Not having a dad proved at times difficult. You wanted to be like everyone else. I did not want to explain why I had no father. The war itself seemed to be a taboo subject. My mother thought there was a pacifist element in a lot of workers mentality and this could be identified in her in-laws and other male friends.

My mother relied on the income from her war widow's pension. Our neighbours all had good incomes, in some cases from more than one earner in each family. It was the case that what other children took for granted, my mother could not afford. Nevertheless, I was oblivious too much of this and thought I had everything I wanted.

My mother had a great sense of humour and saw the sunny side of any challenge. She was a prolific letter writer and corresponded with all her friends, my father's family, on Walney Island and her sisters, on a weekly basis. My mother was different in one other way, she voted Conservative. Why? She said it was the only party that ever increased her war widow's pension.

Mother and father had met in a dance hall in Wigan. He had been born on Walney Island, off Barrow-in-Furness. He had been trained, by serving his apprenticeship in Vickers Armstrong shipyard and attending Barrow Technical College. He was then employed on building a royal ordnance factory near Chorley, north of Wigan.

They fell in love and saved up, finding a house at 153 Shaw Lane, Prescot (situated on the outskirts of Liverpool and south of St Helens). He also had a reserved occupation, meaning he was exempt from war service. They married on the 27 July 1940. They were both ambitious for the future and planning to have a large family.

Bomb Disposal Team

Fate had other plans; between 26 May and 4 June 1940, 340,000 Allied troops were evacuated from Dunkirk, my father's brother Eric being one of them. At this stage in the war, Great Britain, with only Commonwealth support, was at its most vulnerable as America had not yet entered the war. My father volunteered for war duty.

Following training, he was appointed to a bomb disposal team in Swansea. My mother went down to see him for weekends, when he was off duty, and they spent many happy times in Mumbles and other parts of the Gower Peninsular. They planned to go back after the war as they loved the area. Their love letters are tragic to read.

One of his bomb disposal teammates was killed, soon after a photograph of the team had been taken for the local paper, showing all of them with the decommissioned bomb. My father has his right hand on his friends' shoulder, to the left of the bomb. My mother and his wife had met many times and kept in touch by letter for many years after the war.

The family lived in Oldham with their two children, a boy and a girl. Several years later, the boy committed suicide having failed his eleven plus. I remember my mother taking me to their house in Oldham (2 buses and a long trolley bus ride). It took nearly all day to get to their house and after a short stay, we had to leave, to travel back to Leigh.

The war progressed, and in December 1941 the United States entered the war. The 8th Army in the North Africa Campaign required bomb disposal men to deal with Rommel's land mines at El-Alamein. Success at El-Alamein was critical to enable the troops to progress through North Africa, towards Italy and on up to Germany.

I had been conceived on his embarkation leave and this fact became their overriding concern, in their letters up to his death. They planned to have a baby girl, to be called Rita, no name for any boy was considered. My father then spent several months on the deck of an aircraft carrier, going via the Horn of Africa to their first stop in Durban. The Mediterranean was then under the control of the Germans.

I understand that the conditions in the desert were terrible, one cup of water per day and weeks of rat-invested nights, red-hot days and freezing nights. The question was would the troops be fit enough to fight? This will always remain an unanswered question. The mines had to be cleared to allow the tanks through, so it is a futile question for anyone to ask. My father was possibly killed in the battle of El-Alamein on either the 22 or 23 October 1942.

I have all the correspondence between my parents, from the aircraft carrier and his days in the desert. They reveal their deep love and all their plans, based around Rita, the name they had given to their expected daughter.

My mother's grief was palpable, but not without many regrets.

I understand that not many of the sappers survived this early stage of the battle. The Germans had it well covered with machine guns, spraying just above ground level. If a sapper, lifted his head to see the way forward, the intensity of the bullets, could cut it off. I have seen footage from old news films showing the aftermath of the battle with headless bodies being thrown into collection vehicles.

My father had relocated my mother from the house in Prescot to a house in Leigh. Anti-aircraft guns (in defence of Liverpool) had been established near the house in Prescot and he considered this move to be not only safer, but Leigh was a lot nearer to Bamfurlong, where her mother and father lived.

After the War

When my mother had finally decided to take action about the standard of my education, she realised that she needed help writing letters, making a good case and moral support. She approached her four sisters and their husbands for help. Eleanor, her eldest sister's husband, was a strong trade unionist, who replied that there was no difference between his son Frank and her son Walter.

I could see the logic in this, but my mother was determined. I looked up to Frank, like having an elder brother and a good friend. Uncle Frank would not help and a similar response came from the other relatives. My mother's point was, that if my father had lived, he would have ensured that I had a good education.

My mother had taken me on holiday to the Isle of Man (where she had spent her honeymoon) and there she met a man friend called Bill Green. They developed a loving relationship over a couple of years. Bill Green was a travelling salesman, selling gravestones to undertakers and toys to department stores and shops, etc.

From his home in Morpeth, he travelled in a van around the British Isles to all his contacts. He also attended all the relevant trade fairs. He often surprised me with unexpected toy presents from some of these trade fairs.

Bill Green was helpful in supporting my mother in writing the letters and researching whom to write to. Two letters were sent to the Ministry of Defence and both got a refusal. Bill Green pointed out to my mother that the News of the World, had a column called Sir John Hilton's Bureau (1942–1969), that took up cases for people who wanted help fighting bureaucracy.

This newspaper took up my mother's case and I was given a grant for the fees to send me to Bridgewater Independent Grammar School, in Worsley, near Manchester. Unfortunately, the grant did not cover the school uniform or any of the other associated costs. Nevertheless, my mother managed to get employment as a school dinner lady at St Peter's School, several months after I started at Bridgewater School.

The school uniform had to be bought from Henry Barrie School Outfitters in St Anne's Square, Manchester (the offices above this shop became an important destination for me many years later in my career). The uniform and sports gear were all very expensive. The blazer was bright blue with white stripes, so was a large cap, white cricket flannels, white cricket boots, a long bag to carry the cricket gear and football kit. My mother was frugal; I always had a blazer that would last several years. When the teddy boy era commenced, with the long jacket I looked trendy.

Nevertheless, this attire gave me a mental challenge; from my first days at school, I always wanted to fade into the background and not stand out, if possible. The blazer was like having a megaphone to announce my arrival at any destination. I knew I had to be prepared for the stick, on the way to and from school, especially in Wigan Road. (What's in that bag Sharpy? Sharps toffee, I would reply.)

Bridgewater Independent Grammar School had been established by Manchester businessmen, who had not been satisfied with the government's standards of education. The first day at Bridgewater, I was asked by the English teacher to stand up and read to the class.

He quickly asked me to sit down saying, "Sharp by name but not by nature."

My home life started to improve; my mother started a new job in Woolworth's on the hardware counter. That money made all the difference to our quality of life and standard of living.

In the last few years at Bridgewater, I went on organised school trips, camping in Nevin, North Wales, to Austria and my last year to the Olympic Games, in Rome, in 1960. We went to watch Anita Lansbury win the gold medal in the breaststroke final, Gordon Pirie, lapped in the mile, and Brazil play Formosa in a football match.

During this holiday I became friends with another boy from Leigh, Mike Smith and we were close friends, throughout the 1960s, and later, until he died from cancer, in South Africa, in

April 2016. For the last few years of his life, fighting his cancer, we kept in contact on Skype, right up to 2 days before he died.

My mother also had good holidays abroad to Rome, Rimini, Switzerland and Austria, with friends from Bamfurlong and Harbin's Silk Mill, where she had worked as a girl.

My mother's friendship with Bill Green came to an end, when he had put pressure on her to get married. I remember the final act in their relationship. He had asked, for the final time he said, and would not take no for an answer; but there followed a long silence and she continued to read the paper.

My mother carried on reading the paper and he left. Then he returned, setting fire to the paper. A war widow's pension gave security, but she was not going to let the house burn down.

I left Bridgewater School after O-levels, passing in Geography, English Literature and Chemistry and Physics. No English Language or Maths. This result did not make my employment prospects very good!

The 1960s

I did not know what I wanted to do when I left school, so I went to see the Leigh Youth Employment Officer. I was possibly the only lad he had seen that week, wearing a collar and tie. Much to my surprise he sent me for an interview with a small firm of chartered accountants in Cook Street. John Hayes, the senior partner's son interviewed me and offered me a job. I hated it.

It was obvious to all, especially when I started to put my bicycle clips on to go home at about 4:15 pm. John Hayes did me an enormous favour. He had a chat with me explaining that he didn't think that I would make a good chartered accountant and should look for another job. I resisted shouting Hurrah!

In the firm, there was, sat in the next desk to me, a female clerk in her 50s who was friendly and talked about her life. One day, with no encouragement from me, she started to reminisce about her life. She also knew that I was not happy with my job and said I should forget about work and do something in my own time, that I loved.

At St Peter's School, the deputy head, a local celebrity called Tommy Sale had been a professional rugby league player for Leigh. In junior school, he would take my class into Firs Park and pick two teams from the boys in my year, to play tick and pass rugby. I loved it. Rugby has been one of the greatest pleasures in my life, so I did take the advice given by my colleague, in the firm of chartered accountants. Tommy Sale also organised boxing tournaments, in which I was less successful.

The curate at St Mary's Church ran an amateur rugby league team, who played in the Wigan under 17s league. The team trained in the church institute hall, which had a parquet floor, very hard to played 5 a-side rugby on. The first training session involved some exercises and then for the next hour playing 5 a-side rugby.

I was picked for the following Saturday, so started my rugby career. I had not been able to play rugby at Bridgewater as the school only played football. We did not win many games at St Mary's and we were always guaranteed to lose to St Patrick's Catholic Church in Wigan, usually with a few black eyes for our endeavours.

Eventually, the curate left the church and the team folded. Some of the team, including me, went to play for Tyldesley rugby union club. I soon realised that I was not first team material, but I loved the game and was content to settle for the second team. The first team rarely lost a match with some players guesting for some of the leading clubs in the North West.

The first year, I played in the Colts team who also did not lose many matches. I really enjoyed my time for the next few years, playing for Tyldesley. I have lots of great memories from that time. When we played Kendal, we were given a meal after the match and then the coach went on to Morecambe, to the Pier Dance Hall.

On one occasion, my friend Colin Smith, a forward, had his two front teeth knocked out, not a pretty sight in the dance hall. I loved the bonhomie, in the team, singing on the coach, after a few pints, all the great rugby songs.

My friend, Jim Hoffman, who I met when playing for St Mary's, signed professional for Leigh. Several other players also signed for other clubs, so when we met up on a Saturday night, in the George & Dragon, there were a number of professional players in the group.

I remember waiting for my friends to arrive at the George & Dragon in 1963, when Mike Cox came in, asking, "Have you heard the news?"

"What news?"

"President Kennedy had been assassinated."

In July 1962, I organised a holiday to the Isle of Man for ten, all rugby players, including Jim Hoffman, Colin Smith, Frank Raines, Len Owen, Kevin Ashcroft, Roy Camberlin, Roy Morris, Peter Faye, and Roy Healey. The majority are pictured on the following photographs. It was the same week as the Glasgow Wakes week.

One would think that 10 rugby players on holiday would be fairly safe. This proved not to be the case. In every large pub playing live music, we were outnumbered by Glaswegians.

On one occasion, Frank Raines (not a tall man) challenged a very tall man on his way to the gents with the words, "Ha one of the little people," not, in my opinion, aggressive words.

Several minutes later the tall man came out, spat on Frank, and then went round several other tables. Each table downed their pints and held their empty glasses in a very threatening manner. On the count of 3, all ten of us made a fast exit from the pub, through the swing revolving doors, and then split into smaller groups of two or three. We may have been OK at rugby, but we were not stupid.

Left to right—Roy Healey, Colin Smith, me, Kevin Ashcroft, Peter Fay, Roy Camberlin, Frank Raines, Roy Morris and Jim Hoffman

After several days, in the boarding house I came down to breakfast and on my plate was a letter terminating our stay, explaining why. We had arrived at the boarding house early in the morning, after travelling on the overnight boat from Liverpool, having been drinking all night. Our image apparently had not improved over our stay.

There may be other reasons, I could not possibly say, all I will say, is that several Irish girls had become very close to some members of our party. Douglas was very busy, so in order to accommodate all of us, we then had to split into two smaller groups for the rest of the holiday.

Although, several in the party had signed as professional rugby league players, it was Kevin Ashcroft who won every medal there was to win, playing rugby league. Kevin's mother worked in Woolworths and was a friend of my mother. Kevin may have won lots of medals, but on putting lots back into rugby league, Jim Hoffman with Leigh East takes the star prize. I cannot explain how proud I felt when I saw Leigh Panthers run out at Wembley, in last year's Challenge Cup Final, with juniors from Leigh East, running alongside.

The following year, a different group of rugby players went to Ostend for a week's holiday. This party was made up of Jim Hoffman, Mike Cox, Colin Smith, Gerry Hamilton, and Vinney Hilton. The official photographer was Gerry Hamilton, who took lots of photographs, but I later discovered that he never had any film in the camera.

We all had a good time, but it is all now a bit vague now. Although I do recollect that Colin and I did meet two girls from Sedgefield, near Stockton-on-Tees and I did visit one of them several times.

I first met Gerry Hamilton on this holiday to Ostend. He started life as a bricklayer. Not just any bricklayer, he would tell you, having been presented with a silver trowel for his skill. Gerry had been successful in securing a job with Leigh Corporation as a Planner, followed by Managing Directorships with several leading national house builders.

Gerry was then playing professional rugby for Leigh and, when Leigh won, he would be out on the town, in the much-coveted Leigh rugby league blazer. Later he and another friend, Keith Platt, set up a folk club over a public house in the town centre which became very successful. Mike Smith and I had girlfriends, Dorothy and Susan, who collected the door money.

We were let in free, until Gerry found out and sacked them both on the spot. Gerry booked the artists and the venture was a financial success. Gerry did meet Paul Simon, of Simon and Garfunkel, on 8 September 1965, at the Lion pub in Bridge Street, Warrington. He was not booked because Gerry was not prepared to pay for his overnight stay in Leigh.

Whilst Paul Simon was in the Lancashire area, he actually wrote *Homeward Bound* on Widnes Railway Station, the week after he had met Gerry. He must have been inspired by Gerry!

I lost touch with Gerry, when I went to work for Peterborough Development Corporation, in 1972. In 1976, when working for Cheshire County Council, I opened the local paper to see a photograph of Gerry, on the front page, shaking hands with the Duke of Westminster. He was then MD of Barratts North West operation.

I telephoned Gerry and asked for a copy of all the photographs he had taken in Ostend, knowing that they didn't exist. We arranged to meet in my local, the Albion, the next day. This turned out to be the start of a long-lasting friendship. I soon met his wife, Gill, and they met my wife, Kate, and we watched their 4 children grow up. Kate and I became Godparents to his eldest son, Gregory, and we invited each other to important events in our lives.

Gerry went on to become MD of Bellway North West and later MD of one of Trevor Hemming's companies, which specialised in industrial development and the subsequent management of the created investments.

One year his boss, Trevor Hemmings, was raising money for one of Princess Anne's Charities and Kate and I were invited as Gerry's guests. It was £1,000 per ticket and guests brought with them raffle prizes that were auctioned. Kate was told to curtsey, I was told to bow and Gerry introduced each of his guests to the Princess.

When he came to us, he said to the Princess, "What do you think of this bloke?" hitting me in the chest with two fingers.

"He lived in Leigh and then he moved to Chester."

Princess Anne then said, "It is probably warmer down there."

Gerry was always a man of surprises. When he retired to his old farmhouse on the edge of Leigh, he cultivated a large vineyard at the rear of his house. He may yet put Leigh on the map for the quality of his wine. What Gerry would not tell you about is his commitment to the Catholic faith. He is not just any Catholic, but one who has received one of the highest honours from the Pope, the Bene Merenti Medal.

Another Leigh lad who went to St Peter's Junior School was Frank Parr. His brother John was *cock of the school*. I had a playground fight with Frank and Tommy Sale gave us both the cane, in front of the whole school. Unlike Frank, I cried. The caning had not hurt, but it was the indignity, in front of the whole school, that hurt.

Not many years later, Frank Parr played at Wembley, in Wigan's Challenge Cup final, as scrumhalf. I think he was the youngest and smallest player, ever to play for Wigan, in a Wembley final.

I must pay tribute to another Leigh lad who was in the same year at St Peter's School, Clive Powell. Clive was born in Cotton Street, not far from Hulme Road. His mother had died when he was still young and his father had remarried. He eventually became a weaver's apprentice in Hayes Victoria Mill. Clive's aunt had taught him to play the piano and he formed a band, with others in Leigh.

They were popular and toured the local pubs and working men's clubs, including the one near my house in Hulme Road. One year, he was on holiday, at Butlin's Holiday Camp and won the talent contest and was retained for the rest of the season. Clive Powell's stage name was changed to Georgie Fame.

He is still playing, occasionally at Ronnie Scott's Jazz club in London. Gerry and Gill are some of his biggest fans and they have been to see Georgie play there many times. The last time they went to Ronnie Scott's in London, to see Georgie, was in October 2022. They spent half an hour back stage, bringing him up to date on major events in Leigh. If you have talent and are dedicated you can make it big-time, especially coming from Leigh.

At the end of Hulme Road, there was the old farmhouse, whose land had been farmed by the Liversley family. The land was sold to a housing developer, Bushell (a builder from Lytham St Ann's). Further up Wigan Road, another old farmhouse was in the ownership of the Serventi family. My mother rented 12 Hulme Road from Bushell.

This builder had built other housing estates further up Wigan Road, and in Lowton and other parts of the North West. Although, I would not claim that the Bushell houses were perfect, they did have a bathroom and an inside WC. These houses did not deserve the local slang, calling the estate cardboard city. At the time, my father had relocated my mother from Prescot to Leigh, not all houses in Leigh had a bathroom and WC inside. Council houses came along after the war had ended.

Mr Liversley's daughter had married a man called Clark and they had two daughters Margaret and Barbara. The house had a large barn at the rear, a cultivated garden with possibly 2 acres of additional land. At some stage, the land next to the old farmhouse had been developed into two shops, two detached and a terrace of houses.

The shop sold groceries and everything else a family required and was run by Mr Clark and 3 shop assistants. Barbara was the same age as me and we became friends with the other children of similar age in the neighbourhood. The barn and the land were used as a play area and came in useful on bonfire night and on other occasions. The land on the other side of Wigan Road, opposite this farm house, was Marsh's Playing Fields, a very large area of grass, able to accommodate two rugby and two football pitches with land to spare. This site was the location for the regional Coal Miners' Gala in the 1940s and 1950s. Miners, who attended on coaches, came to listen to their trade union leaders and politicians. Tents were erected as beer halls and to serve food. It was possible to listen to the speeches inside our house in Hulme Road. I remember George Brown MP addressing the crowd for over an hour! He was a very popular Labour MP at that time.

The Serventi family was a large hard-working family. The farmhouse also had out buildings and some spare land. Mr Serventi would be called an entrepreneur today. He had several business interests, including delivering firewood in wired bundles, on his horse and cart. This was in high demand from a local population working in coal and getting the coal delivered free. My mother and

Mr Serventi were friends. He always respected her and thought her ability to obtain a government grant for her son's education was laudable.

Many years later, when I had my first car, I garaged it in one of Mr Serventi's out buildings and had it serviced and repaired by a tenant, who occupied another of his outbuildings.

Several of our neighbours, girls and boys, still at school, were forced to be married. At that time, there were no ifs or buts, if your girlfriend became pregnant you had to marry the girl. My mother used these examples to terrify me and made it clear that if it happened to me, she also would make me marry the girl.

This is no longer the case, today men finding themselves in this situation are forced to pay maintenance. They pay 12% of their gross weekly pay for one child, for two children 16% and for 3 and above children 19%. However, this does not guarantee that the father has access to the child. They pay this until the child is 16 or 18 years old. On the 23 June 1960, the FDA approved the sale of Enovid for use as an oral contraceptive, within 2 years it was taken by 102 million women and is now taken by over 3.5 million women.

My mother did encourage me to enjoy life, as much as possible. I was never intimidated by her views. In 1962, I was very attracted to an older blonde woman who caught the same train to Manchester as I did. I thought she had a wonderful figure and I loved to follow her up the steep slope onto the station platform. One day I sat down next to her and our relationship changed and we agreed to meet after work.

She was then 26 and engaged to be married. I was approaching my 19th birthday. We went to a party in Atherton and I took her to the casino and Garrick club. I was upset when she was married and moved away from Leigh.

My attitude, as a single man to the opposite sex in the 1960s, can be summed up as: I love the girls who do and I love girls who won't, but best of all I love the girls who say they won't but look as though they might! My Mother would often quote this ditty to me before I went out to meet my then girlfriend. She loved to tease.

There were many hard-working families living in the Wigan Road area. I will mention one, the large Grainy family. Pat Grainy, often captain of Tyldesley's first team was a coal miner, who with many others, was killed in 1979, aged 40, in the Golborne pit explosion. Tom Grainy, Pat's brother, was one of the first to be appointed to Alec Murphy's training team when he was appointed as Leigh's player captain and coach. Tom also coached me on how to hold a cricket bat on Marshes Playing field, on Wigan Road.

Another Leigh lad was Alan Green who often travelled with me on the 26 bus to Manchester, after Beeching had closed the railway between Leigh and Manchester. Alan worked for Dunlop Heywood, one of the best firms of commercial estate agents in Manchester, at that time. Bob Dyson a colleague of Alan, was the only Manchester agent to persuade me to buy an office block in central Manchester, on a forward commitment basis, for Cheshire County Council's superannuation fund.

When Alan was working for a small property development company, that he had moved to, he came down to Peterborough to assess the viability of buying a department store, owned by a local family. I obtained as much of the development corporation's information relevant to this assessment and gave it to Alan.

Alan eventually went to work for Welmar, the house building company owned by Christian Salvesen, which had been established by Tom Barron (another Leigh lad) when he was senior partner of Dunlop Heywood. Alan later set up his own company of property advisors.

Manchester

When I left the firm of accountants, I could not think of any other way of finding a new job, so I went to see the youth employment office in Manchester. My mother's brother-in-law, Cliff Robinson, was employed by Manchester City Council and he arranged for me to visit. They had organised several interviews for me, one in women's fashion, one in the jewellery trade and one to train as a fire loss assessor and compensation surveyor.

I did not think women's fashion was for me, but I did attend the other two. I was offered the surveyors job with Richard Hoyle & Company, who had offices in St Ann's Square. The building is on one corner of the square and Barton Arcade. Fred Abbott, the owner of the business, interviewed me and appointed me.

It was a very small team at Hoyles, consisting of Mr Abbott, his son Stanley and two other valuation surveyors, Tom Brown and Ken Linfoot. Ken Linfoot, an experienced surveyor, took responsibility for training me. The valuation expertise required included being able to value all types of industrial and commercial buildings, all industrial plant and machinery, on the basis of open market value, going concern value, reinstatement value, indemnity value and scrap value.

A senior valuation and compensation surveyor, Mr Edwards, had died a few months before I was appointed. There was a very good reason why Fred Abbott had kept a small team, which I will cover later.

Richard Hoyle & Co and other similar concerns had been established by the mill owners (the Cotton Barons of Manchester). The Cotton Barons thought they were not receiving full compensation from the insurance company brokers when they had a fire. In the early years of the mills, fires were common. A small metal fragment in a cotton bale could cause a spark when it went through the bale braker, which would then cause a fire. The sprinkler system would then do more damage.

Insurance company policies contain a *Subject to Average Clause* which means that if you are not insured for 100% for the reinstatement value, you will only receive, in any claim, the percentage you are covered for. It is, therefore, important for companies to be fully covered, with annual valuations, if possible.

The two Hoyle brothers, who had established the firm, had volunteered for the First World War. They had appointed a bright young man called Fred Abbott, from one of their mills in Bolton, to run the company until they returned. They did not return.

Other parts of a compensation claim could be loss of profits. This was an area where Tom Brown had made himself an expert and he obtained excellent settlements. He would always have the mill manager on his side and they would prove to be a formidable team.

Tom Brown gave me good advice. He explained that you had to be flexible in your approach to valuing companies and only record the facts that affect value. No point in recording a lavish description of a desk, as it would be a waste of time. He said he had been very successful in settling war damage compensation claims with the government.

He did this by agreeing a method of valuing cotton mills, on the number of spindles in the mill, which reflected the value of everything else, including buildings, plant and machinery, fixtures and fittings etc.

Fred Abbott had expanded the business, by not only acting for most of the cotton combines, but other expanding industries, following the end of the war years. The cotton combines included Fine Spinners & Doublers, English Sewing Cotton, Combined English Mills, and Tootal Broadhurst Lee.

The other industries included bleaching, dyeing and finishing, chemical works, heavy engineering, sewing machine works, whisky distilleries, furniture manufacturers etc. In fact, I cannot think of any industrial concern that they did not value.

I remember on the 10 January one year, in the early 60s, catching the overnight train to Inverness from Crewe, with Tom Brown. We got off the train at Tomatin to value the whisky distillery. We disembarked the train, faced with 5 feet of snow and a treacherous journey to the hotel.

The hotel had only two other guests, custom and excise officers, who with locks and keys controlled all the valves in the whisky distillery process. They did not drink alcohol on the job but made up for it after work. 3 weeks later we returned to Manchester.

Fred Abbott looked every bit the successful Manchester businessman. Starched wing collared shirt, bowler hat and brolly. He also had a red face and robust build. He had been a member of the Manchester engineering club for many years and once a year he would invite other members of the club and other clients to the rugby league Wembley final. He hired a coach and booked a good hotel, in central London, to stay overnight. He did not invite anyone from the office.

I was very fortunate to have been appointed to work for Fred Abbott. I think he came out of the same mould has the Cotton Barons. Fred had been extremely successful, with lots of his clients having London headquarters.

He was possibly one of the last Manchester businessmen to be able to say, "What Manchester does today London does tomorrow."

In 1962, when I had been employed with Richard Hoyle & Co for approximately 12 months, Fred Abbot, then aged 73, sold the business to Edward Rushton Son and Kenyon. Hoyles moved to York house on York Street near to Piccadilly. Rushton's office was on the second floor and Hoyle's office was on the fourth floor.

It was intended that Richard Hoyle & Co would be run as a separate company, in association with ERS&K. The concern that Rushton's, may have had, was that they might start to lose some of the impressive clients they had acquired by the purchase of Hoyles. Major Bill Holgate, who came from a rival company, was appointed to manage the firm and another industrial valuer, Joe Strange, was soon appointed to replace Ken Linfoot, who had then qualified and left to join Manchester City Estates office.

Rushtons organised a day out in Chester, to be followed by a dinner dance at Cotton's Hotel near Knutsford, for all the staff of the two firms to meet.

Ken Linfoot had been a good friend, confidant and trusted advisor and it had been a privilege to share an office with him for the preceding 12 months. Ken was studying in his own time by taking a correspondence course. I knew that Ken was a lot cleverer than I was and I did not think I could qualify by doing

the same, so I had decided to join the police force.

The application forms had been filled in but I did seek his advice. His advice was to start the correspondence course, see how you get on and if it is beyond you, then join the police.

Ken Linfoot and me in York House.

I was also very fortunate to have my mother's financial support. I knew that without her support, I would not have the quality of life that I was then enjoying. Playing rugby, socialising at weekends, wearing a decent suit and travelling to Manchester each day etc.

I was also aware that the prospects of achieving a good salary, before I qualified, were remote. I went to see Harry Kenyon, one of the partners, who agreed to pay for the correspondence course but nothing else. I would not have any time off work for studying.

I signed up for the correspondence course and found that the majority of the subjects were very interesting. Building construction, town and country planning, law of contract, law of tort, law of landlord and tenant, economics and valuation. Bookkeeping less so. I also committed and applied myself to become an industrial valuer.

I was trusted to have my own clients and requested to work with Rushton's industrial valuers on large factories. The clients of Richard Hoyle, with head offices in London, had been transferred to ERS&K's London office. I was also requested to join their team on large factory jobs in London. I often had several weeks, staying at the Strand Palace and other hotels in London.

The clients that Bill Holgate, who he had thought would follow him from Airey Entwistle, did not materialise. So eventually I went downstairs to the second floor to be fully integrated with the ERS&K valuation and auction teams.

The first day, after I had found a desk unoccupied, I heard a voice from the other side of the room with a Wigan accent, "What's this Leigh—doing in here?"

I responded, "Wondering why anyone would employ a Wigan—d?"

There was silence, then Len Walker laughed and conversation resumed. I knew I was accepted. I integrated very well with all the staff at ERS&K. I quickly discovered that on the days in the office, usually on a Friday, when final reports were written up in the office after completion of a factory valuation, my jokes from Leigh were greatly appreciated. The office laughter could often be heard by the senior partners, located in the front of the building.

In 1967, I took my final examinations for the incorporated society of valuers and auctioneers and failed, having failed in two subjects. All the subjects had to be taken again the following year. I realised that if I was going to pass them all, I had to give up playing rugby and curtail my social life at weekends. I did commit myself and passed the final in 1968.

Passing the final coincided with a colleague, leaving from the industrial estates agents team, to set up his own business. I applied for his post and James Rushton, the senior partner's eldest son, after a long conversation, appointed me. Another coincident was that the office in York Street was included in plans to redevelop that part of Manchester, so the office moved to the entrance to St Ann's Square, in Exchange Street.

The building also fronted onto Market Street. This was a more modern building, in a more prestigious address. I was sharing a large office with Dorothy Purdy, a chartered surveyor and experienced marketing expert. The office manager was Harry Whitfield, the partner in charge, James Rushton and one secretary.

Dorothy Purdy had worked with a marketing & design company to ensure that ERS&K's for sale particulars were easily recognised with a logo and had some impact in the market. The firm was already considered to be way ahead of any other industrial and commercial agents in the north of England, in the quality of their particulars. (I attach an example below, the 3 columns fold into a double-sided document, to fit into a slim envelope.)

Back   Front

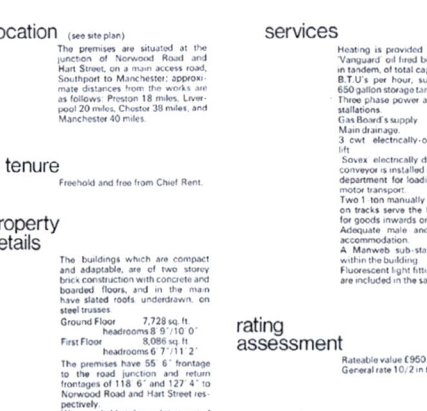

ERS&K had been commissioned by the Secretary of State for Defence to sell the largest complex of industrial distribution properties to be placed on the market in the north of England. The main site in the complex had its own internal railway and connection to the main line. The booklets of sale particulars had already been put together by my predecessor, for which I was extremely grateful.

The first auction took place at the Piccadilly Hotel on the 29 October 1968. Several hundred people were present and a camera team from the BBC. Edward Rushton took bids for about 35 minutes and then withdrew the sale, stating that the reserve price had not been reached.

Edward Ruston, conducting the auction, had not received any bids at all. This information was kept confidential to a limited number of people.

In the afternoon following the auction, three of Manchester's leading industrial agents were invited to meet on the following Monday morning. The agents were Dunlop Heywood, G F Singleton and Robinsons.

They were all asked to bring in a list of all the enquiries they had, for large industrial space in Manchester, to show evidence of demand. Harry Whitfield chaired the meeting and with that information a deal was agreed, at the end of the following week, at the client's asking price. This cooperation by local Manchester agents was not uncommon, if the best interests of Manchester were at stake.

This site is now known as the Heywood industrial estate, Pilsworth. It is located 4 miles south of Bury and 3 miles from Rochdale. It had 5 million sq. ft of existing buildings on a site of

166 acres. It was ideal and became a major distribution centre, being located 8 miles north of Manchester, with unparalleled motorway connections. The motorway connections had not been built when this site was sold but were in an advanced planning stage.

The first sale, that I dealt with on my own, was a builder's yard in Cadishead, west of Manchester. This was quickly followed by 15,814 sq. ft light industrial property in Southport.

One late Friday afternoon, I had a call from Charles Kenyon, the other senior partner (equal status to Edward Rushton). He requested that I go over to Stockport and value an industrial property and report back with my valuation that night. I went, knowing that this could be a test of my ability.

I thought it was a straight-forward job, being a single storey, modern, light industrial property, being easy to measure, including the headroom etc. I reported back with my report and valuation and didn't hear anything further. I concluded that I had passed the test.

After I had been in the estates agency team for about 11 months, my salary had not changed, even though I was doing well, on the fee earnings side. I realised that with my experience, I could earn more working for some other organisation.

I read the Estates Gazette each week and many good jobs were advertised, that I thought I could apply for. I applied for a post with Skelmersdale development corporation and had an interview. This being my first interview, I did not interview well, so cursing on the way home, I knew I could have done a lot better.

Two days later, I was asked to pop downstairs to see Charles Kenyon and found Bill Holgate in his office, as well. I had used

Bill Holgate as a referee for the Skelmersdale job. I did not know, at that time, some organisations took up references prior to interview. I was candid to Mr Kenyon, explaining why I had applied for the job. I said I could not afford to get married.

Immediately they both congratulated me. I said that I had no intention of getting married, I just want more money. Mr Kenyon said that, from his point of view, I would have been worth more to the firm if I had continued to work as a plant and machinery valuer, than working in the estate agency team.

I then applied for a job with Salford Corporation. It was a better paid job, offering a lot more experience. The post was a senior valuation surveyor position, in the valuation section of the city engineer's department. Salford did not take up references until the post had been accepted by the applicant, so when I had the job offer in writing, I gave in my notice to Edward Rushton Son & Kenyon.

Mr Kenyon called me down to his office saying he would match the salary offered by Skelmersdale. I explained that I now had a better offer from Salford and would let him have a copy of the letter of offer and the conditions of service. Mr Kenyon eventually said that it was not possible to match Salford's offer and the partners could not believe the terms of the contract.

It offered flexitime, 3 weeks paid holiday, a grade increasing every year, plus also trade union negotiated increases. They thought it would destroy the salary structure of the whole firm.

Colleagues at ERS&K were eternally grateful, thanking me, for after I had left, a major breakthrough took place with their relationship with the partners.

Las Vegas of the North

Now back to my life in Leigh from 1955 to the end of the 1960s and into the early 1970s. Leigh was transformed, from an industrial cotton and coal powerhouse to a more mixed economy. The coal and cotton industry declined over several years. Mills closed and other industries started to move into empty mills. My mother left Woolworths and started working for higher wages with Ward and Goldstone, an electrical components factory for the car industry, located in one of the mills.

More surprisingly, Leigh itself started to change into a mini downmarket version of Las Vegas. The casino club, in Silk Street, opened in 1955 and attempted to replicate, imitating where possible, the Las Vegas casinos. It was housed in a two-storey brick building, had a large dance floor on the ground floor and a stage which accommodated a dance band.

There was seating around the dance floor and upstairs a balcony, with table seating, overlooking the dance floor. Over the stage was a large room used as a gaming casino, with roulette wheel, card tables etc. The casino was open Friday, Saturday and Sunday nights, with entertaining guests performing during the interval between the dancing.

In the early years, strip tease artists also performed in the interval. The bar remained open until 2:00 am. Eventually, planning restrictions changed some of the entertainment but it still remained

Dancers in the spirit of New Year were enjoying their Leigh Mentally Handicapped Children's Society dance at the Casino Ballroom, Leigh, on Saturday.

a very popular club, until I left Leigh in 1971.

The Garrick club opened in 1961, catering for a slightly different clientele. The owner Roy Jackson had linked up with other clubs in the North West and was able to book acts from a long list of show business stars. Each week the Garrick could guarantee acts from the then current Top Ten. Touring artists from the North America were also booked, and Liverpool and Manchester comedians.

The club was packed at weekends, but less so during the week. I remember that on one Wednesday night, with only a few couples in the audience, watching Sandie Shaw. I was standing near the stage and she seemed to sing to me for 45 minutes, as though we were alone! Sandie then rushed off to her next engagement in Warrington.

The catchment area of the two clubs covered most of South Lancashire, with regular coach trips to Leigh. In the years between 1961 and 1978, entertainers included Bill Haley and His Comets, Del Shannon, Georgie Fame, Gene Vincent, Gerry Lee Lewis, Gerry and the Pacemakers and the Beatles played at the Garrick club.

Coal

I remember when pithead baths were installed in Leigh pits and less black men could be seen on Wigan Road. Nevertheless, a few miners were reluctant to use them. Miners had always, from the opening of the first colliery, been accustomed to going home from the pit covered in coal dust. It was up to his wife to prepare the tin bath, not an easy thing to do without an electric immersion heater to heat the water. The water had to be boiled in a pan on the kitchen fire. The coal dust was also a problem for his wife, the dust went everywhere. Why would some miners do this? I can only guess, the reader should decide for themselves, there could be several explanations. Nevertheless, miners' wives would give verbal abuse to offending miners who went straight home. I

witnessed this on several occasions between the ages of 7 and 9 on the number 3 bus, which travelled up and down Wigan Road.

Leigh buses were not like the majority of buses provided by local authorities. The upper deck did not have seats for two but had a side aisle with bench seats to accommodate up to 6. You could get trapped at the end of the bench, next to the window.

I have already stated that my grandad, William Hall, had been a coalface worker, in a Wigan colliery, so it was only natural that I should follow the coal miner's relationship with the government with interest. The coal miner's strikes have often, in my opinion, been distorted by the media. The BBC, even in 2022, represented Arthur Scargill as a hero doing his best for the miners. I will deal with the facts as they relate to me and my mother.

The dispute between the government and the coal miners started as a normal strike in 1983, as the strikes before, but the reluctance of Arthur Scargill to have a ballot created friction between the different coal mining areas. It set coal miner against coal miner and the unfortunate deaths of miners crossing picket lines.

If you wish to learn the truth about the Thatcher years, you should read the three books by Charles Moore, The Authorised Biography of Margaret Thatcher, the miner's strike is covered in volume two.

Arthur Scargill was not Joe Gormley.

When the miners' leader Joe Gormley died, most of the British press wrote an obituary on his life. They all treated him with respect and even the right-wing papers accepted that, although he had led two miners strikes, in 1972 and 1974, he was mainly credited with bringing down the Heath government. Nevertheless, Gormley led his miners back to work with a big smile on their faces and the best paid workers in Britain. Some press called him wily Joe for his negotiation skills.

The miners, then 240,000 strong, emerged from the strikes with dignity and money.

What is not generally known is that he influenced the miners pension fund to invest millions in the north (in accordance with their investment criteria).

In the 1960s, the coal industry employed the largest number of men, more than 300,000 nationally and it was one of the largest employers in Leigh. Working in the pits caused my grandad's early death and the burning of coal had a detrimental effect on air quality. In October 1966, a coal slag heap at Aberfan in Wales slipped, engulfing a school and killing 116 children and 28 adults.

Coal slag heaps were common in the Leigh and Wigan area and the surrounding districts. At the end of Hulme Road was Giggleswick flash, a coal subsidence lake. At the far end of the flash was a large area of slag heaps, with one over 170 ft high. This was called the Yo-Yo and it was a challenge to climb, not only because it was steep, but also your foot could slip down into hot smelly pit slag.

This area was for me and my friends an adventure playground. Damming the run-off streams from the flash, after heavy rain and fishing in the flash and the two Tunnicliffe Weaving Shed reservoirs were popular pastimes. In summer, the reservoirs were used as a swimming pool with hot water running down a shoot from the mill.

Nevertheless, thank God, we never experience an Aberfan in the Wigan and Leigh area.

Smog in the area, prior to the introduction of smokeless zones, lasted for days, with visibility restricted to only several feet. If you had a weak chest, it could cause other breathing problems and it affected those who had to travel to work or school. Unfortunately, the coal seams under Leigh and that part of Lancashire had pockets of methane gas which could explode, killing many miners if any spark occurred.

Eventually the uneconomic pits started to close and the unemployed miners were helped by the government to secure new jobs. Miners were very proud of their occupation and were very reluctant to move to a different way of life. Nevertheless, an average of three miners were killed at work each week and my grandad was one of many to die of its industrial disease. My mother was determined that her son would not be going down any coal mine.

Before I return to my career, I must inform the reader of Eunice and Arthur Hood, who had an important influence in my life. Eunice had become a widow, early in her married life, and had to bring up two small children and look after her father, who was dying of silicosis.

From being small, my mother had taken me to 28 Lily Lane, Bamfurlong, to see her mother and father. We visited them most weekends. When we arrived at their home, we would have a cup of tea and catch up with Nana and Grandad's life and other gossip. Following lunch, we would walk over the railway bridge to the rest of the village and to Eunice's house.

The house was a typical miner's terrace cottage. It had two bedrooms upstairs and two rooms downstairs. The front room was never used, kept for special guests (who possibly never arrived). There was an outside WC at the end of the yard, a coal shed and a tin bath hanging on the back wall. The back room was for everything else a family needs to do.

A Yorkshire range with fire oven combined used for cooking and a kettle for continuous cups of tea and other uses. Eunice's father's cancer was at an advanced stage and he sat next to the fire, spitting black phlegm into the fire and coughing with nearly every breath. Eunice also suffered from psoriasis and often shredded dead skin onto the floor. It was not a situation I looked forward to.

Nevertheless, my mother always seemed to be in a party mood and entertained all for the next two hours. I was a reluctant participant.

Several years later when the children had left home and married, Eunice's luck began to change. Eunice had always been a member of the Church of Christ and in her mid-50s, she had more time to become involved with church work. Another member of the church, Arthur Hood's wife had been seriously ill for some time and Eunice helped to nurse and support her.

Following Arthur's wife's death, Eunice and Arthur's friendship developed and they were eventually married. Arthur had a car and Eunice learned how to drive. Arthur and Eunice became frequent visitors to our house in Leigh. Arthur had worked, as a young man, in the drawing office of a Glasgow shipyard (learning to be a marine engineer) and in his own time he had studied, at night school, to become a school teacher.

He had left the shipyard in his 40s and progressed in the teaching profession to become deputy head of Wolverhampton Technical School, before he retired. I enjoyed talking to Arthur and we became great friends. He had given me a reference for the job at Salford, as did my friend, Mike Smith's father. They were both chartered engineers by profession.

My mother was diagnosed with cancer, not long before Christmas, in 1970. Eunice and Arthur gave priority support to me and my mother, visiting at least twice a week. Eunice did my washing and, more importantly, kept my mother's spirits up. They promised my mother that they would continue to give me their support after her death. This meant so much to my mother, coming from her best and her most loyal friend.

Eunice, Arthur and Lawrence, taken just before Arthur's 90th birthday, 28 July 1980

Life as a Local Government Officer

I started at Salford Corporation, in August 1969, at the same time, as two senior valuers were leaving and one had already left 2 months before. This left in terms of the valuation staff, Bill Simcock, the section head, Stan Wood and myself. It then took several months for the full complement of new staff to be recruited. A deputy for Bill, three senior valuers and a junior estate management surveyor, plus another building surveyor.

Stan Wood and I agreed to work overtime for 4 days a week to keep the ship afloat. We had a break for half an hour, after normal hours, to have some tea in the canteen and then worked for about another two and a half hours. We decided what work had to be prioritised and what could be left for a later date.

The strategy was to try to meet the council's requirements with the limited resources we had. It was not difficult, as Stan and I were both experienced valuers and knew how to take short cuts to arrive at a valuation. For example, central government had requested a valuation of the council's housing estate. There was no way we could do an individual survey and valuation of each property.

We tackled this by dividing the estate into blocks of each area of the city and by driving round each area, agreeing an average high and low value for each property, taking account of usual valuation considerations. Back in the office we double checked the figures, with reference to the evidence we had of sales in the open market. This resulted in less than 3 weeks work, rather than at least 12 months.

The valuation section was not based in the town hall. It was over an electricity show room on the corner of Bexley Square, fronting onto Chapel Street, one of the main arteries into Manchester from the west. All the team of 15, except Bill Simcock, were housed in one room. The majority smoked cigarettes and 3 smoked pipes. It was a smoked filled room, always noisy, very hot in summer and very cold in winter, with inadequate heating.

The room was not large to accommodate the existing staff and the new arrivals, to be recruited for the increasing workload. The plan was to move to new offices in Water Street, a building previous occupied by the water board. In October 1970, I went on holiday with Mike Smith to Majorca and when I returned to work, a week before the office move, a new girl had arrived in the office.

A new compulsory purchase technical officer had arrived to replace the one who had returned to work for Manchester City Council. Kate Maguire was wearing very unusual stylish glasses. The next week we all moved to Water Street.

Stan Wood and I were soon joined by other valuation surveyors, namely John Bruton, Tony Higgins and Tim Foster. We were in one room upstairs and Bill Simcock and a secretary were in separate offices. Downstairs the property management team, terrier clerk, two CPO reference officers were in one room and three building surveyors in another room.

Outside was a car park and an outbuilding, that we converted into a games room with a table tennis table and darts board. The building was some distance from the town hall and this isolation encouraged us to possibly take advantage of the situation.

The mail was delivered to our office and the legal conveyancing section, in another out post, by a man called Vince, who had lost an arm in the war. Vince liked to call into one or two pubs on his round and with a large leather bag, he carried over his shoulder.

One day the bag got caught, in the swing doors of a large public house, in Bexley Square. The more he pulled at the bag, the more it wouldn't move, until the city engineer, who was talking to John Bevan his deputy, rescued him. Not a pub he would visit again!

Whilst the office was still in Bexley Square, before the new staff arrived, Stan and I could choose which committee we would work for. The choice was education, slum clearance, highways, estate management or housing. Stan chose slum clearance work and I chose highways.

I made the right choice, as this made me responsible for buying the property and land for the M602 motorway and the A6 improvement scheme. John Bruton chose education, which was also interesting work, buying property for new schools.

I remember this being a very happy period. The whole team enjoyed their work, lots of jokes, and long lunches in the many pubs around Water Street. A pub only 25 yards from the office, on the other side of Chapel Street, was frequented by George Best with his latest girlfriend and other M/C United players. Also, the cast of Coronation Street would often pop in for a drink. Bet Lynch wearing hot pants was a sight for sore eyes!

From 1969 until 1971, when I left Salford, the two road schemes

I was dealing with had been given outline planning consent, but the compulsory purchase orders had not been approved and notice to treat had not been served.

This meant the property required was blighted, as the owners could sell, but would not receive the full compensation and legal and agent's fees would not be paid. Going concerns would not receive disturbance compensation etc. This was not just. The law was changed a few years later.

I also had an advantage in my negotiations, the district valuer, acting for the Inland Revenue provided me with all his evidence of recent transactions in the area. Although the situation did not seem fair, the Inland Revenue had to frank all the purchases the council made.

I gained a lot of experience during this time, buying a lot of large going concerns and lots of houses. The largest industrial property being Taylor Crane's, required for the A6 improvement scheme.

Terminal Cancer

In December 1970, my mother was diagnosed with terminal cancer. The cancer specialist at Wigan infirmary, Dr Silva, explained to me that my mother would not live very long, but he was prepared to treat her with a relatively new course of drugs, called chemotherapy.

This treatment could extend my mother's life, hopefully for another 12 months. I agreed to this proposal and signed the forms of approval. I had a telephone installed at home and paid a lady to come to the house each day to look after Mum and keep me informed, whilst I was at work.

My mother's health deteriorated, she lost a lot of weight, had difficulty in keeping food down, retched and was often sick. The shock of losing all her hair proved to be a big challenge; wearing wigs did not go down well, but she did wear them.

I had a long talk with Bill Simcock, my boss at Salford, who gave me his support and said he would be as flexible as possible, if I could carry on working.

I had then been dating Kate Maguire for several months and said I would commit to only dating her, but my mother's health would be a priority for the rest of my mother's life. I also cut social contact with all my normal circle of friends.

In the summer of 1971, my mother's health improved, so much

so that Kate and I took my mother to Blackpool, with a friend, for a week's holiday. My Auntie Mary and her sister, my Auntie Winnie were then sharing a house in Blackpool, and they all met up and had several nights out together. Having settled them in Blackpool, Kate and I went to the Lake District for a holiday, picking them up in Blackpool, on the way back to Leigh.

The extra year that my mother lived, was important to me. She was my best friend but during that time, we became even closer. Although she had brought me up as a Christian and the local vicar visited, she confided to me that she didn't believe in the afterlife.

One day, in late October, my mother asked me to take her to Walney Island to see the relatives, but not to stay overnight. We set off in my red mini up the M6 and onto the coast road to Barrow-in-Furness. When we were about half an hour from Walney, she asked me to stop at a road side cafe for tea.

We had tea and then she asked me to take her home. I said it was ridiculous to turn back now, but I did. It was many years later, that I realised she never intended to visit any relations. Spending 3 hours in the car with me, was all she wanted.

My mother died on the 15 December 1970. Kate helped me to organise the funeral service at St Peter's Church and we booked the Co-op restaurant for the wake. Kate being a first soprano with the Manchester Halle choir, sang at the service, an aria from the Messiah, "He shall feed his flock" (soprano part) with a local pianist.

The church was full, and many came to Wigan Crematorium before we went to the Co-op for the wake. Later that day I drove relatives back to Sale and went for a drink with Uncle George,

Auntie Lily, Auntie Edna and her friend Norman, who she later married. On the way home, we had to pull off the motorway and I was very sick outside Worsley Court house.

I was so lucky, my mother was not only my best friend, but she kept me on the straight and narrow path with many pearls of wisdom for any situation you might find yourself in. Examples are a stick in time saves nine, a rolling stone gathers no moss, all work and no play makes Jack a dull boy, fortune favours the brave, if a jobs worth doing it's worth doing well. There are lots more.

It was not long after meeting Kate in Bexley Chambers, that I asked Kate for a date. I had been elected as the trade union representative for the department (Bill Simcock's secretary, Joy, had put my name forward). I took my responsibilities seriously, attending the conference in Blackpool one year and meetings in Salford. All the office was going to a NALGO social evening, so I asked Kate to be my guest.

I had left-wing views at this time. I had voted for Harold Wilson and to this day, still believe he did a good job. Harold Wilson had kept the country out of the Vietnam war and this, I believed, was one of his major achievements. There were certain aspects of Rushton's (ERS&K's) management of its workforce which I thought demeaning.

The annual salary increase involved the senior partner, Edward Rushton, going around the firm at the Christmas party. To each member of staff, he gave a slip of paper, with their weekly salary increase shown. This included men in their 50s, as well as the junior typists.

The other thing that got under my skin, was having to call the partners sons Mr James, Mr Brian, Mr Alan, etc., even if they were younger than myself. I had no problem with any of them as individuals, treating them all as equals, telling them the same jokes, I told everyone else.

Many years later, I did realise how important the 9 years with Richard Hoyle & Co and ERS&K had been. I would not have been able to progress in my career, in the way I did in the 1970s.

Taking a correspondence course to qualify, at the same time as gaining exceptional professional experience, enabled me to apply for positions that had been advertised on the basis that only graduates need apply.

At any interview, the important question is, "What experience do you have, to do this job?"

However, I did drop my left-wing views after leaving Salford.

The NALGO social event was the start of my love affair with Kate Maguire, which did lead to a wonderful marriage, but not without an uphill struggle, at the start.

Kate had a strong ambition to join the Halle choir, as a first soprano, and following a stressful audition was accepted. I didn't know at the time, that Kate would introduce me to classical music and that it would give me so much increasing pleasure throughout my life.

Fate played a part in Kate coming to Salford. Kate had applied for a post with her then employers, Cheshire County Council, which had an essential car users' allowance. This would have helped her to pay for and run the car she had purchased.

The senior officer, following the interview, told Kate that she had given a very impressive interview, but he could not possibly give this job to a young lady. Kate applied for the same job at

Salford with the same car allowance. The difference between rural Cheshire and Salford is stark, for referencing land and property for compulsory purchase.

I had been thinking of my next career move, for several months, before my mother's diagnosis and I had become increasingly interested in New Towns. My colleague, John Bruton, and I had been to a presentation in Preston regarding the proposal to develop the Central Lancashire New Town.

We both thought that this proposal, in this location was wrong. Spending the amount of capital required, would be better spent in the opportunities existing between Liverpool and Manchester. There was in this area, already a skilled labour force going through structural change in employment.

I put this forward at the meeting, but no support was forthcoming. Nevertheless, I did want to obtain New Town experience and applied for a job with Peterborough Development Corporation when it was advertised in the Estate Gazette in early 1972.

The chief estate surveyor, John Case, interviewed me, with his assistant chief, Paul Dowsett, and his chief administration assistant. I had stayed in Salford overnight and travelled down to Peterborough, early the next morning and came back the same day. I returned with the good news that I had been offered the job, subject to references.

I was still recovering from the death of my mother, at this time, but also wanting a new challenge in a new environment. This was a difficult period for both Kate and me. I had not, at this stage, proposed to Kate, even though it was at the forefront of my mind.

I wanted space to think, to master the new job and know that

I had made the right decision, to leave the town of my birth. I did propose later that summer and we became engaged and set the date to be married for the 23 December 1972.

Kate is a committed and practising Roman Catholic. For many years, she played the organ at St Werburgh's Church in Chester and was the choir mistress. I have always been sceptical about an afterlife but considered the church's teaching (ten commandments etc.), to be good guidance for a happy life. I had no problem, in telling Kate, I would give 100% support to her Catholic faith.

When I eventually proposed to Kate Maguire, I had no shadow of a doubt that she was the girl, I wanted to spend the rest of my life with. We were married at St Werburgh's Church, in Chester, on 23 December 1972

Peterborough Development Corporation

This was the government's case for the new city. Faced with tremendous pressures for expansion in London and the South East, the government decided in the mid-1960s to divert population and employment to new cities. These were to become big enough to be regional centres in their own right, and they were far enough from London, to become effective countermagnets to the pull of the capital.

As a result, Peterborough Development Corporation was set up by the government, in 1968, to carry through the rapid and largescale expansion of Peterborough, in partnership with the city and county councils.

The area of the new city of Greater Peterborough is 15,940 acres. The population increase was to be nearly 100,000 from 88,000 in 1970, to about 188,000 in 1985.

The aim was to not just to create a greatly enlarged and prosperous manufacturing centre. It was to create a new regional capital, with the widest possible range of shops and services and a high proportion of employment, in offices and with offices, providing services for national and international markets.

Peterborough was already a major communications centre at the crossing point of the main north-south and east-west routes. The main railway lines and the A1 (the Great North Road) linked

London and the north and the A47 and the railway lines, between the midlands and the east coast, were the main routes.

It was thought that as Greater Peterborough grows, the city's rise as a regional employment, shopping and service centre could be spectacular. No less spectacular would be the city's rise as a regional centre for sports and recreation.

The development corporation was primarily responsible for the planning and development of all the expansion areas, where most of the 100,000 new population would live. It was also taking the initiative in planning and redevelopment of the city centre, which would be the dominant commercial and administrative centre of the region of over 400,000 people.

Instead of the continuous extension of the built-up area as found in other cities, it was intended to build four distinct new townships—Bretton, Paston, Orton and Castor. Each would house approximately 30,000 people.

When I started at the Corporation, in 1972, the Bretton Township was substantially developed. In the first few months of my arrival, a Sainsbury's superstore opened in Bretton retail centre. This opened up a new way of shopping for families, allowing them to do a weekly or monthly shop, in one shopping trip. Each township would be built in succession (except Paston, which was more infill than green field development).

The four townships would be closely linked with one another, with the city centre and other employment areas, and with the national road system. The plans for Bretton had only been approved by the Ministry of Housing and Local Government in June 1970. I thought it was remarkable what had been achieved so far.

In Bretton, every home in the township was able to have central heating, but none would have a heating boiler! There was one central boiler (with back up boiler) providing all the hot water needed for every home, primary and secondary schools, and all the shops, offices and social centres.

It was also intended that Nene Park, running along the valley of the winding River Nene, would be extended from the A1 to the city centre and the river embankment.

Plan of Designated Area

My Job at Peterborough

My job was to buy all the land and property for the Orton Township, the second to be built, and ensure that the compulsory purchase order, was in place to serve notice to treat at the required time.

I was also given the job of buying the Nene Valley Railway (John Case saying it would keep me busy for the next 10 years). This purchase was to provide the local Nene Valley Railway Society with the line to operate steam trains, to and from Wansford Station, which had recently closed. Other duties included representing the department, on the Orton project team and the housing for sale project team.

During the period of serving notice with Salford City Council, I was able to think about the options open to me, for buying or leasing, a property in Peterborough. I had taken out, 2 or 3 years before, a policy with the Prudential, an Insurance Bond called *Young Man in a Hurry*.

This policy was aimed at people like me, who may wish to convert the policy into something else, at a later date, maybe an endowment policy. It would work for buying a house, on the basis that the capital growth of the endowment policy, would cover the cost of the mortgage by the time it matured.

The interest rate was fixed and the premium per month, for the mortgage, was less than one would pay per month for the mortgage.

It was risky but paying less per month with the possibility of making a capital profit, at the end of the mortgage, on a 25-year term, seemed to me to be a reasonable risk.

In this period, I also discovered that Bert Bullough and his wife Mary Baxter, had moved to Peterborough and Bert was working for the development corporation, in the planning research team.

Bert was born on Wigan Road and brought up about 100 yards from where I lived. I telephoned Bert and they invited me down to Peterborough to get familiar with the area and sort out a property to rent from the DC. I drove down to Peterborough and stayed overnight and the next day I arranged a development corporation house to rent.

I also put £25 deposit on a plot of land, where the local builder was proposing to extend the new housing, in the village of Longthorpe. The contract fixed the price of the house at £7,600, which would be payable on completion. I considered this to be a remarkable deal! The economy was already experiencing inflation. I considered that, if the builder started on site now, it would take more than 6 months to build and the open market value, could be a lot more on completion.

Bert and I had a chat about how the DC worked and I told him what my responsibilities would be. He then went for a copy of the local paper, to show me an article, he thought would be of interest. A farmer, in Orton, had taken offence at a large timber post and sign erected on his land, notifying that this land was subject to a compulsory purchase order.

He had taken the post and sign into the development corporation reception area and thrown it at the glass screen in front of the receptionist. No one was hurt, but this information did give me time to think about the reception I might have, and how I would deal with the land owners.

I commenced employment with the development corporation on the 22 May 1972. Paul Dowsett took me around the estate department, introducing me to the staff, who all made me feel welcome. Paul then told me about a priority job, that had been awaiting my arrival.

The job was to do a financial appraisal of all the proposed use, of all the land in the new Orton Township. This was the last anyone saw of me, in the estates department, for several weeks. The completed job was handed to the finance department, to complete a submission to central government.

In June 1972, I started to concentrate on my work priorities and found that I did not need to worry about the attitude of local farmers to the compulsory purchase of their quality farm land. I had met two well connected local individuals, who did the marketing for me of the DC's intentions.

The first was a county councillor, who Kate and I had met in a pub in Wansford. I had been recommended the pub, for the quality of the beer. At 10.30pm, when last orders should have been called, the landlord locked the front door, played dance music, started to pull pints and serve other drinkers.

After another half hour, two police men knocked on the front door and were each served a pint. They should have been policing the A1, in a patrol car. I started a conversation with an elderly man, with a large moustache, who wanted to know where we came from. He said he had recently been to visit a modern prison, between Warrington and Leigh, on County Council business.

The county were considering giving planning consent for a

similar one. He wanted to know how I would be able to buy the land, in Orton, with such local opposition. I explained that the compensation payable to the land owners, would possibly change their minds, when they understood the full package.

A very generous valuation of the quality agricultural land, full disturbance compensation for relocation and roll over tax relief would be payable. This would enable the farmer to relocate anywhere in the country, with good quality farm land, like Lincolnshire or the Cotswolds etc.

Several weeks later, I received a telephone call from the Secretary to Lord Fitzwilliam's estate, who lived in a cottage on his estate. She was very well connected around Peterborough. I drove out to meet the lady, an elderly spinster, for afternoon tea. Over tea and homemade cakes, we developed a friendship. I explained that I was not expecting any problems with any farmers in the designated area, as the acquisition from the DC would be generous.

If there was a feeling that farmers would be out of pocket, perhaps she would pass my message on that this would not be the case. We kept in touch, so much so, that when my son was a few months old, we visited for afternoon tea and cakes.

It proved to be unnecessary, over the next 2 years, to visit individual Orton farmers, in their properties. They would telephone me, in the office and I would explain the likely compensation they would receive, in broad terms. Once they had agreed, I would report to the DC board.

The next stage was to instruct the district valuer's office to negotiate the detailed heads of terms and take the transaction to completion. This was a much better way of dealing with the transaction, than at Salford, where I was personally involved with all the detailed negotiations.

The Nene Valley Railway proved to be a bigger headache, initially. I sent several letters to York, the railway estate office, responsible for selling the land and track, with only an acknowledgement for a reply. In the engineer's department at the DC, Roger Mann, a member of the railway society, was employed. He had asked several times how the negotiations were going. Roger Mann and I met to discuss whether there was any solution.

We came to the conclusion that I should write to the railway engineering department in Derby. I wrote and Roger and I went to Derby and met two engineers and agreed to buy the track. Roger had obtained a lot of information about the track and the advice was that it was valuable and suitable for main line use. We were both bowled over that we had done the deal, at a very reasonable price.

The railway society was also delighted. They applied for a Light Railway Order, which would take some time, but in the meantime they were able use their steam locomotives (already acquired) on the track, but only for maintenance work.

Paul Dowsett and I had a very good working relationship. He was the chair of the housing for sale project team, and I was on the Orton project team. He pulled my leg about the north. He thought that all Northerners kept pigeons in their back yard, coal in the bath and lived on a diet of double pie and chips. We also, discussed many things in his office and planned the important points we wanted to have debated.

We both thought that the housing estate layouts, on the Rathbone layout system, was not what most house buyers wanted. It meant that the houses would front onto landscaped walkways, with no road access to the front of the properties, only access through to the back door, meaning access for visitors, would be through the kitchen.

Also, building to Parker Morris standard meant that the cost of the house, would be more expensive than the equivalent private sector property. Builders build to match buyer demand. The demand was for houses with a front drive and garage at the front, possibly to show off their new car, not having it hidden away at the back.

The DC houses ticked all the right boxes from a planners' and architects' position. The points, I made at the project teams, led to complaints to John Case about me. I must have had some support on the department's management board, for I don't recollect any criticism. Also, Wyndham Thomas had given a speech to staff, that he wanted contribution from all at the project teams, saying that we are all planners, on the teams.

I also thought that the DC policy of meeting the need to complete the development, as quickly as possible, did not achieve full value. Especially, in the case of housing and the sale of land. In one case, it was decided, by the board, that the DC would sell 40 exclusive, individual house building plots, in Bretton Woods. This was to provide houses, at the top end of the market, for future executives.

I had no problem with the proposal, but putting all the plots on the market, on same day and making them available to in-house staff, would not achieve best price. Nevertheless, they were all sold and developed quickly, even though a strict developer's brief had to be met.

The overall objective of the DC was to provide social, and the full range of houses, including attractive property, for chief executives of major companies moving to Peterborough.

Deals were also done with national house builders, with a large percentage discount, on the land value, on the basis that the land value would be subsequently clawed back, by the DC, on the selling price of each house. This created competition in the market with many builders on site. Speed being a more important consideration than full value.

Kate and I had agreed to visit each other at weekends. I would drive up on a Friday night, after work (a 3-hour journey) and drive back on Sunday night or leave Salford at 4:00 am on Monday morning. This was exhausting and on one occasion, on attending an important meeting at 9:00 am, I had to excuse myself and to go to the WC, once in the WC, I fainted.

Nearly half an hour later, I went back to the meeting. (I never found out whether I missed anything important). The meeting had been with Neville Smallman, the DC Solicitor and Roy Ashton, chief assistant planning officer. The meeting was to finalise the land to be included in the Orton CPO and the land to be excluded.

It was clear that Neville's focus was to exclude as much of the land as possible, in the two Orton villages and Roy's focus was to include as much land as possible. I had taken Roy's side in the discussion for the land remaining in the villages would not be in the DC's control.

Kate visited Peterborough when she could make it into a long weekend, by having Friday and Monday as leave. We became engaged on the 28 July 1972 (having bought the ring on the 22 July) celebrating with Kate's mum and dad in a hotel in Crewe.

Travelling up to Salford on the 18 August, on a Friday night, I had a bad car accident on the outskirts of Worksop, ending up in the local hospital. Rodney Barlow, my proposed best man, came with Kate the next day and took us to Kate's apartment in Salford. The car took until 2 weeks before our wedding to repair, with a delay of several weeks to obtain a special jig, to be brought from France.

I was fortunate that the Renault 16, was built like a tank, as the car had rolled over in the accident. Today, the car would have been written off and I would have had a new one.

The period before our wedding without a car was difficult. It was always more difficult to travel east-west on a Sunday than north-south, by train. When I went up to see Kate after August, until we were married, it sometimes took 5 hours to get back to Peterborough on a Sunday evening (sometimes sitting on Nuneaton station for up to two hours awaiting a connection). The railways, at that time, did most of their maintenance work on Sundays.

When it became known that I was getting married, I came under pressure to organise a stag do. Several colleagues had suggested that the best place to go was a night club in Leicester, so I organised a coach to take us to the club. I quickly had a full coach. It turned out to be a great night out, and the subject of conversation for the next month or so.

At the end of the night, the coach driver dropped each person off at their homes. It was unbelievable service. I paid for the cost of the coach, even though my boss had signed the invoice; thinking it had been required for a business trip.

The structure of the estates department at Peterborough was different to most DCs, as it did not have a deputy, but three assistant chief officers, responsible for each discipline. My boss, Paul Dowsett, was responsible for land acquisition, housing for sale and management.

Dick Harvey was responsible for the sale of industrial land and development, and Kenwyn Brown, commercial. Each department had a senior estates surveyor (my title) and other qualified staff as required. In April 1973, the assistant chief industrial, Dick Harvey, had accepted a job with one of the London Estate Agents and his job was advertised. I wanted this job and applied for the post.

I realised that, if I was successful, it would commit me to Peterborough DC for several years. Unfortunately, I was not successful, and the job was offered to David Parr, who had been working as senior industrial estate officer with Runcorn New Town.

I enjoyed my job at Peterborough and made many good friends. Nevertheless, I had wanted New Town experience on my CV and after 2 years, I had it. I wanted to move back up north and had started to read the Estates Gazette with renewed interest. Kate concurred with this view. She was missing the Halle choir, and her parents were in Crewe, a 3-hour car journey away. It was far from perfect.

In November 1973, a Senior Property Consultant's job was advertised in Manchester, with Property Development Service, at a starting salary of £5,000 (a rate of pay, for my experience, only available in London). I applied for the job and at the interview I discovered that the company only had one client, the Cooperative movement!

Property Development Service was managed by Frank Williamson, who had worked for the Cooperative movement all his life. He had applied for the job as head of property at the co-op but had not been successful. He was known for having left-wing sympathies and wrote articles for the Morning Star. The co-op wanted to keep him as they thought he was exceptionally good at his job.

He offered to stay on one condition: that he could set up an independent consultancy and achieve for the movement, what was beyond the co-op's ability at that time. They were not represented in new major town centre shopping developments, had very few superstores and often were unable to secure planning consents.

The co-op sponsored lots of Labour politicians at local and national level. They would have had to declare an interest and would not have been able to vote on planning matters. The image, at that time, was not good from a retail point of view, nor were the co-op societies financially sound. All the retail societies were independent of CWS, operated as friendly societies and they were not PLCs, so the market was suspicious.

I had no knowledge of the Cooperative movement, except as a boy, shopping with my mother, in one of its stores. However, the librarian at the DC had worked for the CWS and was able to provide information on the movement and lots of up-to-date information on retailing, shopping trends etc. This information not only helped me prepare for the interview, but also to research specifically retail development issues.

Paul Dowsett was also very helpful. He had worked for Corby New Town and a colleague of his, David Askew, had left to join Property Development Service in Manchester. Paul rang David Askew, who told us that he had been recently asked to resign from PDS and was taking them to an industrial relations court.

He said the job involved a lot of driving, he had driven 35,000 miles in the previous year and spent, on average, 2 nights a week away from home. The company cars provided were death traps and one new employee had walked out the same day he started. David also said PDS paid high salaries but messed about the individual afterwards.

He had recently secured a new job, which had been difficult to find, after working for PDS. Nevertheless, he thought the job was interesting and would give lots of experience and responsibility, to anyone prepared to take the risks involved. After this conversation with David Askew, Paul said I must make my own decision on the move to Manchester.

I was fully prepared for my interview with Frank Williamson, in new century house, Manchester, in November 1973. Confirmation that the job was mine with a new company car and other safeguards (following the views of David Askew). I gave notice to the DC and started in Manchester on Monday 11 March 1974.

I received a very kind letter of thanks from John Case.

Greater Peterborough

W R Sharp Esq
10 Yew Tree Walk
Longthorpe
PETERBOROUGH PE3 6NT

Peterborough Development Corporation
Peterscourt Peterborough PE1 1UJ
Telephone 0733 60311 Extension **151**

Your reference
Our reference   EST-1/JC
Date   7 March 1974

Dear Walter

It was no surprise when you told me in January that you had been successful in obtaining the post as Property Development Officer with the Cooperative Wholesale Society Limited in Manchester.

I certainly cannot let you leave without expressing my thanks for all the work you have done. I hope you will look back on some of the issues you have handled and the problems you have solved with some satisfaction. I am sure you will always think of the deal you did with British Rail in the Nene Valley, and perhaps there might be an occasion when you will be permitted to travel on one of the steam trains! The other job which springs to my mind is the Omnibus CPO, and I recognise the effort and the experience you put into this. At least you can leave with the knowledge that a major referencing task has been satisfactorily completed, and that this in turn led to the purchase by agreement of perhaps 2,000 acres.

I know you are moving into a fresh field of activity, and I have no doubt that you will succeed in it. I hope your new job gives you the kind of experience you are seeking, and that you find it satisfying and rewarding.

If you think I can be of any help to you in the future please do not hesitate to let me know.

Yours sincerely

John Case

General Manager Wyndham Thomas   Chief Estates Surveyor John Case BSc (Est Man) FRICS

Property Development Service

Frank Williamson's team comprised four property development officers, each with a target of £20,000 PA in fees to earn from the retail societies, in their allotted geographic area. This seems a small amount today, but in 1974 it was not. Each PDO had an assistant surveyor and there was one experienced management surveyor.

This was the total of the professional team, plus three secretaries. We could also call on specialist advice from the architects' department and a site assessment team.

My job involved advising retail societies on all property matters, handling negotiations for major town centre schemes, acquisition of superstore sites, arranging finance and acting as project manager and coordinator.

I was very successful in the 2 ½ years I worked for PDS. I did achieve the required £20,000 fee income and more. The other three PDOs operated in a different way from me. One was politically motivated and used the Labour party connections, to gather information and influence. It worked for him.

The other two were site finders. I had worked with planners at Salford and Peterborough and knew that the local authorities should be the first port of call. Initially, I would write to the head of planning and meet one of his senior officers, before I went into a prearranged meeting with the chief executive of the retail society. It was always going to be to impress them, so that they couldn't risk not employing you. I knew CWS was not always considered a friend by the societies.

My successful property development achievements for the co-op, were as following:

1. A major town centre scheme in Lincoln, with a superstore on the ground floor, next door bus station (part of the scheme), parking on the roof of the store with trolley travelator access into the store and apartments overlooking the river Witham.
2. An 80,000 sq. ft district centre in Sinfin Moor, Derby.
3. The purchase of town centre stores in Nottingham, Northampton and Norwich.
4. I also acted for Mr Cook, chief executive of the Greater Peterborough Cooperative Society, in securing the Orton Township superstore.

I was fortunate to meet Peter Neary, from the architects department, who like me was very interested in all planning matters. He had an ambition to have a sabbatical and take a degree in planning. The Lincoln scheme had to be won by tender, from the Lincoln City Council. Peter and I wrote the brief, under the supervision of Stan Betts, the Chief Executive of the Lincoln Society. We were both delighted when we were successful and Stan Betts took us, with our wives, out for a meal in Lincoln.

Eddie Allan, who had worked for Asda for many years, was head of the site assessment team, and without him and his team,

I would not have been so successful. Not all societies would appoint Eddie's team as they thought they did not need their help.

Frank Williamson, when briefing me on the societies in my patch, told me not to waste my time with Derby Society. He and other senior managers agreed with his view, that Derby Society was heading for bankruptcy. They had been selling their assets to stay in business, for several years.

Nevertheless, I had been working on a letter which I was intending to send to the head of planning in each area, where opportunities existed for new co-op superstores. I could not see a problem with sending my letter.

I had a favourable response from Derby City Council and a good meeting with the deputy chief planning officer. The first statement he made was that Derby co-op and the council were not on speaking terms, so it was good to meet with someone from head office.

I did not respond by asking why but said I could not become involved in local politics. I explained that the co-op movement was moving direction by investing in modern superstores. He asked a planning colleague to joined us, who revealed all the retail development opportunities around the city.

One opportunity made me very interested indeed. It was a proposed district centre site at Sinfin Moor, a residential expansion area, south of the city. Outline planning consent had been granted and Edward Erdman, London Agents, had been appointed to find a developer.

The next day I booked an appointment with Derby co-op's chief executive. Mr Barford had just returned from a 3-week holiday abroad and was in a good mood. When we met in his office, I explained my brief from CWS. The main thrust was to develop modern superstores of approximately of 50,000 sq. ft with a minimum of 500 car parking spaces. I asked if the society had any such plans?

He thought that the way forward, would be for me to sell the proposal to the society's board. A date was made for me to attend a future board meeting. The next day I rang Edward Erdman and made arrangements to meet the partner dealing with Sinfin Moor District Centre.

I eventually received the board's approval to negotiate a deal with Edward Erdman. I had, by this time, been told by Erdmans, that Asda was also interest in buying the land. They required Asda and me to bring our best offers, in writing, to their London office. I telephoned the society and arranged a meeting to agree the figure.

I had prepared a residual valuation (which included the open market value of the completed superstore, less all the costs of development, including finance, fees and construction costs etc). I was aware, by now, that the society did not have the financial resources to build and retain the freehold of the superstore. I had explored finding a developer, to build and lease back, the completed building.

I also suspected that Asda may not be interest in the development. I thought that if they had been, they would have already been on site by now. So, I had prepared another residual valuation, on a worse-case scenario.

The society agreed that I should attend the meeting, taking the two letters with me, one in my inside pocket and one in another pocket. I attended the meeting in London, taking the society's building manager with me, as a witness and to remind me of the right pocket. Asda didn't show.

The purchase of the land was completed. I had been told that the best deal for financing the development could be with Charles Street Builders (Leicester) Ltd. I had a meeting with Mr Murphy, the boss, in his large office, with several clocks on the wall behind him, with a different time on each.

Mr Murphy ran an international business, not just in construction. No time was wasted, he wanted to progress the meeting. We agreed the specification of the building. I thought I would struggle with expensive requirements e.g. the sprinkler system, marble entrance hall, etc. He agreed to everything.

I also thought the rent would be expensive, but it was not. The only stipulation he made was that I would have to use his architect. I was pleased with this decision, as it would relieve me of all the bureaucracy of using the CWS architects department.

The Chief Executive of the Peterborough Cooperative Society had retired, some months after I had joined PDS. I decided to visit the new man, Mr Cook. My main reason was that I was not happy with the secretarial support in Manchester. It took time to have my letters typed in Manchester and often I needed to dictate them and leave the office, days before they were typed. Many mistakes had been made.

Mr Cook had been recruited from CRS; a special society set up to operate bankrupt co-op societies. The individuals involved had to be hard and ruthless, restructuring the failed society quickly to create viability. Vast parts of England and Scotland were now run through CRS.

I spent most of our meeting telling him about PDS and what I had in my plan. He was interested, so I knew he thought he could benefit from our relationship. I then requested that the society do my typing, and could I park my car on their car park? Mr Cook agreed to the arrangement, on condition he billed CWS for the cost. The benefit to him, he would be able to read all my mail!

He said it was essential that he secure the Orton superstore and wanted me to advise.

I had been with Frank Williamson, to see the Chief Executive of Nottingham co-op, and had been introduced to their building manager, Ray Foulkes. The society had recently opened a new department store in the new Arndale Shopping Centre. The society had owned part of the site of the Arndale.

The building manager had been responsible for the fitting out work, using Howard Sant partnership design practice. I suggested to Mr Cook that I take Wyndham Thomas, the development corporation's chief executive, to meet Ray Foulkes, to show the quality of a co-op development, by inspecting the department store. He thought this was a good idea.

A date was arranged to visit Nottingham and along with Wyndham Thomas, John Case, the chief estates officer, came along. I thought Ray Foulkes did a good presentation and the visit had been a success, but no comment was made by Wyndham. It took some considerable time for the co-op to secure the Orton superstore, but they did.

The area I had been allocated to earn fees, included the East Midlands and all East Anglia. There are not many superstores in this patch. Peter Neary and I decided to take up the challenge by doing presentations to societies, in an area that may benefit.

I remember going to Beccles Society on 10 February 1975.

There was thick fog, on the day, and we nearly drove into a dyke. The societies boardroom was full, but we were not sure that this was the best use of our time.

I stayed with Eunice & Arthur in Hindley, near Wigan, on Monday nights. After leaving Leigh, they visited Peterborough often, with Eunice driving carefully all day to arrive safely. My mother would never have believed it.

I made many friends with all the chief executives of each of the societies I acted for, and many of their senior staff.

I received several letters of thanks when I left, and many saying, "Keep in touch."

I didn't think that we would work together again, 11 years later!

**North East Midlands
Co-operative Society Limited**

Registered Office: Cromford Road
Langley Mill
Nottingham
NG16 4EA

Telephone: Langley Mill 3011-3 (3 Lines)
3083-9 (7 Lines)

Nottingham Road,
Ripley, Derbys.
Tel. Ripley 2183.

23rd July, 1976.

Mr. F.B. Williamson, ARICS,
Manager,
Property Development Service,
C.W.S. Ltd.,
P.O. Box 53,
New Century House,
Manchester. M60 4ES.

Dear Mr. Williamson,

       It was with pleasure that I met you personally for the first time at Stanford Hall this morning, it is always pleasing to meet with someone with whom you have spoken and corresponded over the years.

       I must reiterate my sadness at the loss of Walter Sharp from your staff and if it was only a question of salary that has taken him from you then the C.W.S. have done the wrong thing. Nobody carried the Co-op banner more strongly than Walter, nobody could have been more loyal to yourself and the C.W.S., and nobody could have done a better job for Retail Societies. I hope it will not be too late when you realise the significance of this loss because it will have a profound effect upon your department and its co-ordination with Societies.

       Even at this late hour it would be worth any effort you can make to retain Walter Sharp. I sadly fear that his step is irrevocable, but if not, then it is worth another try. You will never replace him fully at the several Societies where I know of the esteem in which they hold him.

Yours sincerely,

W.H. Brighouse.
Chief Executive Officer.

LINCOLN CO-OPERATIVE SOCIETY LTD
SILVERGATE HOUSE · 32 CLASKETGATE · LINCOLN · LN2 1JU

TELEPHONE 26421
10 LINES

SB/JH

PRIVATE & CONFIDENTIAL

23rd July, 1976.

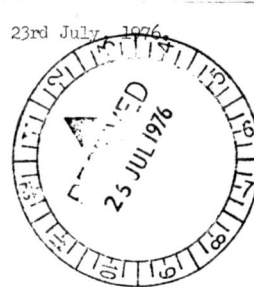

F.B. Williamson, Esq., A.R.I.C.S.,
Manager, Property Development Service,
Co-operative Wholesale Society Ltd.,
P.O. Box 53,
New Century House,
Manchester, M60 4ES.

Dear Mr. Williamson,

    I was indeed sorry to receive your letter, reference FBW/CR/4392, dated 13th July, 1976, upon my return from holiday informing me that Mr. Walter Sharp's resignation had been accepted by your Department.

    It is not, of course, for me to interfere with the staff whom you employ in your Department, other than to say how pleased I was that you were able to send people of the calibre of Mr. Walter Sharp and Mr. Peter Neary to conduct negotiations with the Local Authority on behalf of my Society. I know that the Local Authority was impressed with them and it was very pleasing to me to see the way in which they conducted themselves in the meetings that we have held.

    I am concerned that in an expanding Department such as your own that professional young men of this calibre are allowed to terminate their employment, not because of dissatisfaction over pay but because there is just no career structure available to them.

    As you will doubtless be aware, the developments undertaken by the Leicestershire Society and, more recently, by the Derby Society with Mr. Murphy have resulted in a number of Chief Officials approaching Mr. Murphy with their own particular Superstore problems. His reputation for completing a Superstore in six months from start to finish in these days of inflation cannot be ignored. In contrast with this the Lincoln project has already been deferred from an opening date originally envisaged to be in November, 1977 to April, 1978, and when we were asked at the recent meeting with the Council what date we would commence on site they were told we should like occupation on 6th January, 1977. I have since been approached to see if we can once again defer this date and I must insist that the January date is strictly adhered to.

Cont'd ....

F.B. Williamson, Esq., A.R.I.C.S.   2.   23rd July, 1976.

    I will have to satisfy the Local Authority that the development will proceed in accordance with the time schedule which has been agreed with them and must be assured that the Lincoln scheme takes its priority and is not held back because of new work that may be accepted by your office. It would be a tragedy if anything should go wrong at this juncture due to matters over which I have little control and I must express my uneasiness and ask you to pass on my anxiety to whoever may be responsible.

    I would add that during Congress I was approached by the Chief Official of a large Society and a C.W.S. Director with regard to my dealings with your Department, and if the same question was put to me at the present time my answer would be more guarded than the one previously given.

Yours sincerely,

Chief Executive Officer.

Why did I leave? I realised that the work with PDS was an opportunity to obtain experience that would complete my CV and present a more secure future. I had put everything into this job. I was often working a 12 hour day with long-distance driving. I had fainted several times. I thought the job could possibly give me a health problem.

My son had been born, prematurely, on 11 October 1972, at 30 weeks and kept in intensive care for several weeks. I was missing everyday contact with Kate and my son, Lawrence. I had been leaving Peterborough at approx. 4:00 am, on a Monday morning and often not returning home until Friday. When I did do some work from home, Manchester would telephone at any time, sometimes up to 9:00 pm.

I also thought, *All work and no play made Jack a dull boy.*

Cheshire County Council

One weekend in the summer of 1976, we were visiting Crewe, to see Kate's parents. I had brought with me that week's copy of the Estates Gazette. The advertised job was chief assistant development surveyor, in the county valuer's department, of Cheshire County Council.

I thought I had to apply for this position, not only for the family's benefit, but the post fitted all my experience, to that date, and I knew I would have a good chance of winning the position. Kenwyn Brown had recently been appointed as county valuer. I had not had any dealings with Kenwyn at Peterborough, but he was on the department's management board, and I was proud of my record at Peterborough.

"The Devil you know is better than the one you don't," another saying from Mum.

The county land agent had retired in 1975. John Boynton, chief executive, and John Kellet, county secretary & solicitor, had persuaded the Conservative administration to replace the head of property with an experienced commercial valuer. The reason being, that in the next 10 years, the county would be declaring a vast amount of property surplus to requirements.

Also, the investment panel for the county superannuation fund had decided that it wanted an exposure to property investments. Kenwyn Brown, from Capital & Counties, was appointed as county valuer. I was subsequently appointed as chief assistant development surveyor and had to appoint a new team, to deal with the growing work.

Prior to starting with Cheshire, I was asked to attend a meeting at county hall, with Healey & Baker, Peter Winfield, H&B's senior partner and another partner David Wheeler, who was responsible for a team of investment surveyors, to finalise the terms of their appointment, as advisors to the superannuation fund. The county valuer would act as joint advisor with Peter Winfield. I was surprised at this, it gave Kenwyn Brown the best of all worlds, and wonderful opportunity for me.

I was very grateful that for the next 11 years, that Peter Winfield and David Wheeler and members of his team, were very generous with their advice to me. John Greenwood H&B's industrial expert had stayed with me overnight, when we both gave a talk to ACES on industrial development. (ACES will be covered in depth in the appropriate chapter.)

My role was to work closely with the investment team at H&B and have my own contacts in the development and investment market. We did a lot of forward commitments with developers for the fund, to secure prime industrial and office schemes. This enabled the guarantee of the building specification, the lease terms, level of rent and any sharing of rental overage, split on completion of the investment.

When proposed tenants had been identified, I instructed the county treasurer's department to have a Dunham Bradstreet report, on the covenant strength of the tenant. It was important that the tenant was able to meet the obligations in the lease, on full repairing and insuring terms, upward only rent reviews every 5 years etc.

On starting at Cheshire, two officers were transferred from the county architect's department into my team: John Wood, an architectural technician and Karen Towers, a section clerk. They were both very good members of the team, who gave me wonderful support.

My life would have been very difficult without them both. Karen stayed in my team until she married and moved to Manchester and John stayed in my team for 11 years, until I left in 1987. John had a great sense of humour and the loudest laugh in Cheshire.

The first professional surveyor to be appointed, was known to Kenwyn Brown, when he had been with Capital & Counties. The interview proved he was the best candidate. Mike Perkins had already had a lot of investment experience, having worked for Cinven, the British Coal pension scheme. Other professional staff were appointed as the work increased.

One of the files given to me, in the week that I started with Cheshire, was of a property on Eaton Road. The property had been inherited by the city council, some 13 years previously, from a local industrialist Edward Peter Jones. The property was in a trust, controlled by the Charities Commission, which stipulated that the property was to be used for training of young people in good citizenship.

The property had been passed to CCC on local government reorganisation when education passed from the city council to the county council. The building was by then dilapidated and the land behind the house, extending to over 8 acres, had become a jungle. I went with John Wood to inspect.

I knew what to do with the land and how to reinstate the building. I recently had the experience, at Peterborough, of selling 40 individual, residential building plots at Westhawe, in the Breton Township. I still had a copy of the Development Brief, but I would not be selling all the plots on one day.

I applied for planning consent, and this was dealt with by the County Council, as land owner. My application was turned down, with several reasons for refusal. On the edge of the Green Belt, visibility splays on Eaton Road and Structure Plan reasons. I considered one reason to be valid. The visibility splays on Eaton Road. Looking towards Chester on leaving the site, the road did not have good visibility. The County Council were still working on the 1976 Structure Plan.

I decided to appeal on behalf of the Charities Commission. This would have been the first test for the new Cheshire County Structure Plan. John Boynton summoned me to his office to discuss the matter. The County Planning Officer, with one of his assistant chiefs was present, and one of the senior solicitors. I was asked to present my case.

Then John Boynton requested that I leave the meeting. The next day I received a telephone call from John Boynton. Submit another planning application, was the message I was hoping for. This one was approved.

The best 4 plots, with good views of the river Dee, were selected for sale by auction. I appointed Swetenhams, as selling agents, the largest firm in Chester. The main reason for selecting this firm was that they had an exceptional auctioneer, mainly employed for selling cattle. We booked the largest room, in the Grosvenor Hotel, for the auction. I had put my credibility on the line. Everyone thought, including John Boynton, that the development brief would put everyone off, but I knew that it had worked in Peterborough, and it would work in Chester.

Mr Schreiber, a furniture manufacture, acquired the first two adjoining plots. He was building a factory in Warrington New Town and wanted a northern home.

We released 4 plots to the market, when each phase of houses where nearing completion and looked good. There was no need to have any more auctions. This continued until all the plots were sold. At the same time, work was being carried out on refurbishing the house, called Greenbank, which was to be a catering college. The house became a good restaurant for training chiefs and waiters and was very much enjoyed by local residents.

The county did make a lot of property surplus to requirements. On being declared surplus, I inspected and if I considered it had any development or investment potential, it was placed in an investment portfolio called the Corporate Estate.

This not only created an investment portfolio but also supported economic development in Cheshire. My team also worked closely with the planning department's economic development team, to build small business centres across Cheshire. This included a large building owned by Shell, in Ellesmere Port, which was surplus to their requirements.

Les Rogerson, deputy solicitor, and I, had many meeting with the chief executive of Stanlow Refinery, to set up ENTEP properties, whose building fronted the M53 motorway. A manager was appointed to let the small industrial units and give advice to new businesses. I attended the ENTEP board meetings, when I was working for Cheshire, but also many years later when I was working for Ellesmere Port.

Crewe Business Park was created from the surplus land, of the Crewe & Alsager College. I was told that the district council, also had surplus land, at the rear of this land. I went along to see the chief executive of Crewe & Nantwich Borough Council, to sell the proposal of building a business park. Crewe's land was land locked, so the county had to be the driving force.

The retired marketing director of Warrington & Runcorn New Town had set up a small consultancy in Chester, called Loines Furnival. Mike Loines had also worked for London Docklands development corporation, and he became part of our team. He advised on the marketing, corporate identity, brochures, publicity, advertising, exhibitions, signing and various aspects of the development.

We had a small, landscaped lake at the entrance. The infrastructure, lake, road and landscaping work were undertaken by Crewe and the county provided the development, project management and valuation advice. Crewe appointed John Dunning to coordinate for the Borough Council and John Ashton represented me.

John had joined my team from another section in the valuers department, wanting more experience. The private sector did the development of each phase of the business park, building on behalf of occupiers, or speculatively and letting the completed building.

Crewe Business Park Development Team

The county also had acquired land for road and schools, which sometimes did not go ahead, presenting other development opportunities. One was Stanney Ten, at Junction 10 on the M53. This site presented an opportunity to build quality flexible industrial units (planning B1 space). The specification of the building was important, and I wanted to build a development that the county could retain.

I had the confidence to know what would work, but how would I finance the development? A tax-based lease, lease back deal, the financier factoring in the industrial building allowance which was available at that time. A financier, Joe Dweak, had been into the office and explained this method of funding to me.

It involved the county taking a 13-year lease from the financier, at a fixed rent, which would be less than the open market rent. I was confident that Stanney Ten would let reasonably quickly. The financier would pay and employ the developer/builder. Joe Dweak appointed a company from Preston to build to my specification and provided the finance.

When my section clerk had moved to Manchester, I inherited a new section clerk, Pauline Randles, who was transferred to my team from Kenwyn Brown. Pauline saw the benefits in the relationship of the team being involved in property investment and development, networking and the promotion of Cheshire, without being told.

Pauline recommended that we should take the opportunity of opening Stanney Ten with a bang. The bang would be inviting Debby Greenwood, the current Miss Great Britten winner, to cut the ribbon at an opening ceremony and inviting all the property commercial agents in Liverpool and Manchester and the important councillors from Cheshire and Ellesmere Port. This is what we did.

The photographs tell the tale. I picked up Debbie on the day, so that I could brief her on what was important. Debbie had to chat to all the guests and be photographed with them all. I knew I would not need to give Debby a lift home, she was in demand, and it was not long before Debbie was on TV.

From L to R—The Mayor of Ellesmere Port & Neston Borough Council, Labour Warrington councillor, Basil Jeuda, Labour leader of the County Council, Debby, the Mayor's wife, Kenywn Brown, the county valuer and me.

L to R—Debby, The Mayor of E P & N, Stephen Ewbank, chief executive of E P & N, Fred Venables, Labour Leader of E P & N Borough Council.

My Team

L to R Anthony Milne, John Ashton, Debbie, John Wood, Pauline Randles, and me.

I do not remember any of my work having to go to any committee. The purchase of investments for the Cheshire county council superannuation fund went to the chair of the investment panel. This was by letter to Councillor Ribbeck, delivered by hand, setting out all the heads of terms and a full brief of the property and proposed tenant etc. I was grateful to John Boynton and John Kellett setting up systems to obtain quick decisions when they were needed.

One of my successful schemes was the redevelopment of a dilapidated office building, on Lower Bridge Street, in Chester. I had done the deal with Pochins, a builder and developer based in Middlewich, Cheshire. The property had a listed façade, and the rear walls would have fallen down, but for substantial raking timber shores, holding up the back walls.

After Pochins had spent a large amount on building steel support to the front walls, they realised they had a problem. They had discovered that the lintel timber support, above the front windows, in the brickwork of the facade, turned to dust. It was not possible to retain any of the front walls of the building. A structural engineer was employed by Pochins, to prove it was not possible to retain the facade. Several weeks later, on a bank holiday weekend, Pochins demolished the front walls of the building.

On the Tuesday morning, when I came into the office, Jeff Cross, the conservation officer for Chester, was standing in the centre of Lower Bridge Street shouting at me, he called out 'county council vandals!' An enforcement notice was served on Pochins, which stopped work on site.

It took several months, after going to the court, for Pochins to return to the site. Work on site continued, and about 2 months before completion, Mr Kellett summoned me to his office, to tell me that it had been decided, that the council wanted to keep the building. Fortunately, we had an option in the deal to buy the building on completion.

It was a stroke of luck, that it had not been a county council project, dealt with by the architects department. It would never have been redeveloped with the problems experienced by Pochins. The old Ursuline Convent building, Dee House, turned out to be a good example of how not to deal with a listed building.

It stands there, for all to see, on the site of the amphitheatre, in the centre of Chester, some 30 years plus, after it was vacated. This building although dilapidated, is still in a lot better condition, than the one in Lower Bridge Street that we had to deal with, then called Richard House.

The convent building, when it was in good condition.

The county owned a 37 acres site at Ann Street Widnes, which was than the subject of a Derelict Land Reclamation Scheme, sponsored by the department of the environment. The first 10 acres phase of the Bowers Business Park was to be developed as a retail warehouse park. This 10 acres' phase was placed on the market in April 1986.

I had been involved with the county's Derelict Land Reclamation Team and the district council prior to the land going on the market. However, I was then able to delegate this work into John Ashton's capable hands.

The property investments for the superannuation fund, had grown considerably over the 11 years that I had worked for Cheshire CCSF. The last valuation in 1986, by Edward Erdman, the independent valuer, is set out below:

CHESHIRE COUNTY COUNCIL SUPERANNUATION FUND

SCHEDULE

NO.	ADDRESS	TENURE	VALUATION £
PROPERTIES HELD AS INVESTMENTS			
1.	ANDOVER, Hampshire Plot B5 West Portway Industrial Estate	Leasehold (approx. 120 years unexpired)	385,000
2.	AYLESBURY, Bucks Aylesbury Industrial Centre	Freehold	1,170,000
3.	BURTON-ON-TRENT, Staffs Clarke Industrial Estate, Wetmore Road	Freehold	850,000
4.	CHESTER, Cheshire 4 Watergate Street	Freehold	200,000
5.	DUDLEY, West Midlands 44/45 High Street	Freehold	1,000,000
6.	DURHAM, Co. Durham 22/23A Market Place	Freehold	1,500,000
7.	GLASGOW, Scotland 114/140 St Andrews Road	Heritable	335,000
8.	GLASGOW, Scotland 222/224 West George Street	Heritale	425,000
9.	GREAT YARMOUTH, Norfolk 29/30 Market Place and 18/21 Market Row	Freehold	825,000
10.	GUILDFORD, Surrey 120 High Street	Freehold	1,600,000
11.	HANLEY, Staffs Units 1 and 2, York Street	Freehold	300,000

NO.	ADDRESS	TENURE	VALUATION £
PROPERTIES HELD AS INVESTMENTS			
12.	KINGS LYNN, Norfolk 141 Norfolk Street	Freehold	650,000
13.	KINGSTON-UPON-THAMES Surrey Nos. 40C, D and E, Clarence Street	Freehold	2,150,000
14.	KINGSTON-UPON-THAMES Surrey 59 Clarence Street	Freehold	2,650,000
15.	LEEDS, West Yorks. Unit 2, Benyon Park Lowfields Road,	Freehold	350,000
16.	LEEDS, West Yorks Phase V, Millshaw Park Industrial Estate	Freehold	250,000
17.	LINCOLN, Lincs 314/315 High Street	Freehold	1,625,000
18.	LONDON EC4 4/7 Red Lion Court	Freehold	2,500,000
19.	MANCHESTER Greater Manchester Queens Court, 24 Queen Street	Freehold	850,000
20.	PLYMOUTH, Devon Phase II, Newnham Industrial Estate	Leasehold (approx 116 years unexpired)	295,000
21.	PLYMOUTH, Devon Phase III, Newnham Industrial Estate	Leasehold (approx 117 years unexpired)	290,000

NO.	ADDRESS	TENURE	VALUATION £
PROPERTIES HELD AS INVESTMENTS			
22.	ST NEOTS, Cambsire 3, 5 and 7 High Street	Freehold	750,000
23.	STOCKPORT, Greater Manchester, Retail Warehouses Georges Road	Freehold	1,850,000
24.	STOCKTON-ON-TEES, Cleveland 129/130 High Street	Freehold	650,000
25.	SUTTON, Surrey Benhill House 12/14 Benhill Avenue	Freehold	625,000
26.	TORQUAY, Devon Broomhill Way Industrial Estate	Freehold	1,000,000
27.	WARRINGTON, Cheshire Units 4A, B, C and D, Barley Castle Trading Estate, Stretton	Leasehold (approx 995 years unexpired)	600,000
28.	WESTON-SUPER-MARE, Avon 43 High Street	Freehold	535,000
29.	WIGAN, Greater Manchester 31/33 Market Place	Freehold	800,000
30.	WILLAND, Devonlace Willand Indsutrial Estate	Freehold	265,000
	Properties held as investments - total		£27,275,000

In March 1981, I was requested by the county emergency planning officer, to attend a conference at the Home Defence College at The Hawkhills, Easingwold, York, from the 23 to 27 March. I think I was the only representative from local authorities at this conference, as all the other delegates were senior police officers, at chief inspector level and above.

The conference was to prepare senior police for their designated duties in the event of a nuclear war. The conference covered all that would happen, following a nuclear strike. The delegates were split into 5 groups of 11, with a good mix of officers from all over the UK, in each group.

There were several scenarios of what would follow the first strike, as the situation changed for the worst. From the first day of the conference, the police took issue with the military's advice. The policy was to stay put, in other words all residents would be told to stay at home and stay under the stairs, or in another location that would protect you, if the building collapsed.

There was film showing what could happen and an exercise on a nuclear attack on a major city. We soon worked out that it was Nottingham. The first strike would be at high level (stratosphere) knocking out all electronic communication.

The next strike would do all the damage, and most would not survive. Those who did would experience major problems, which seemed to be the survival of the fittest. Law and order would collapse. The major issues were examined: radiation, high casualties, public morale, looting, communications etc.

The police response was that initially they would arm themselves and there was no way they would be stopping the public from driving, as quickly as possible, into the countryside, out of the major cities. There would be no prosecution service, so it would be 3 stripes, blue, yellow and then red, applied by un-washable paint on to your head. The 3rd stripe would warrant shooting, as there would be no prison service.

The best part of the conference was listening to the police, in the bar at night, reminiscing of their experiences on the beat. Looking back today, when it appears to me a more dangerous situation than at any time of my life. Are we more, or less prepared today than we were in 1981?

From 8 February to 5 March 1982, I was privileged to go to Ashridge Management College in Buckinghamshire, on a senior management development course. The other delegates were a good mix from private sector industry, several bankers and 5 Libyans.

A lot of the course work was business related and small groups were given exercises in competition. We had one weekend at home, in the middle of the course and one Saturday we took the college coach to a London night club.

The Ashridge College Delegates of March 1982

The county council had, for the use of Cheshire schools, an outward-bound centre at Plas Newydd, on the Isle of Anglesey, which John Wood encouraged most of the team to attend, each October. It was a chance for the centre to entertain (terrify or kill) county staff. We arrived on a Friday afternoon, after tea and after settling in the dormitory, we went by boat across the Menai Strait, to a public house on the far shore. This was a must, whatever the weather.

The next day, we had to choose which of the activities we would do for the weekend. The choice was either sailing dinghies, mountaineering or canoeing. The instructor would guarantee, that whichever one you chose, you would remember the experience. I think they compared notes afterwards.

On the Saturday night, it was always a curry and you learned not to ask what the ingredients were! Some people would say the weekend was good for bonding the team! Survival would be a better term. Nevertheless, over the next 11 years, I didn't miss a trip.

My Local

I have had a local pub in every town that I could call home. In the early 1960s, it was the George and Dragon in Leigh. It was the first port of call on a Saturday night, where I would meet my rugby playing friends, before we went to one of the local hot spots.

Later in the 1960s, when I had a car, it would be the Jolly Carter in Lowton were I would meet my friends, not all male, and then drive to a night club, to anywhere within an hour drive. The choice of club was improving all the time. In Peterborough, my pub was the Fox & Hounds, a 5-minute walk from our house in Longthorpe.

However, it was only when I arrived in Chester in 1976 that I entered the pub of my dreams. The Albion in Albion Street. In choosing a local, it is important that the pub serves at least two quality beers and is recommended by CAMRA (the campaign for real ale). It is also important that the landlord must have the same ideals as yourself, on what a pub should offer. The Albion ticked all the boxes.

Mike Mercer is your man, but Mike died 2 years ago, a few days before he had been landlord for 50 years (such is fate). However, a lady came to the rescue, Mike's wife Christina is the new landlord and is doing the job as good if not better than Mike.

However, still with Mike's dry sense of humour, the sign on the bar with the words 'This week's guest lager—I can't believe it's not p—' is still there. It did not stop lager drinkers from buying it and drinking the ghastly stuff.

You will not find in the Albion a television screen or hear piped music. What you will find in the Albion is memorabilia of the first World War, in every room, to honour those who willingly gave their life for their Country. Regulars loved Mike's Trench Nights, a black-tie formal dinner, when we stood to attention to sing to the music and then listen to the poetry. Also, his curry and jazz nights were equally popular. The local press wrote a good obituary but the most eloquent was Professor Glyn Turton's, that appeared in the Guardian Newspaper, on the 17th November 2021.

I agree with all that Professor Glyn Turton says in his obituary of Mike Mercer, but I would add how Mike protected the space for the drinker that no other landlord in Chester would ever contemplate.

He banned those people attending Chester Race Meetings by locking the front door of the pub and regulars had to walk down the back alley to enter through the kitchen. There was always a sign at the front of pub banning stag nights and hen parties, babies were band and so were under 18s, so were small portions, no chips, it was mash.

Nevertheless, the food provided by his daughter, a trained chief, was very popular. It was the best liver and mash with vegetables and thick gravy you could have in Chester.

Mike was an uncompromising man of few words, you either liked him or did not. I have now been a patron of the Albion for 48 years, so there must be something I liked about Mike.

My wife on leaving West Cheshire College and I had our leaving parties from work in the Albion, in the large room behind the bar with a roaring fire. I think Kate obtained a better discount on the wine than I did. This room when I first joined Cheshire was a games room with dart board for inter departmental matches. I have many good memories of nights in the Albion and I hope many more to come.

Group Development Manager CWS

In mid-summer of 1987, I received a telephone call from Malcolm Clark, an old colleague from PDS in Manchester. Malcolm had been promoted to general manager, the top position in property group. I had kept in touch, in fact, on two occasions he and Frank Williamson had tried to tempt me back to PDS.

He asked if I would join him and his personnel manager for dinner, at a large hotel near Warrington. I thought it would be good to be treated this way and have a night out on the co-op. Malcolm was offering me the job of group development manager.

All the buildings, south of logo, where occupied in 1987 by CWS, more have been added.

The proposed job would make me responsible for all property development nationally and joint company operations. The salary would be a big increase for me and there were many perks, including a top of the range company car and very good expenses. It would also include membership of the British Council of Shopping Centres, with the attendance at the UK conference and the European conference (held each year in a different European City). I was interested.

The personnel manager said that at this level of appointment, the CWS required all group managers to be tested over a 2-day period, to include psychrometric testing, presentational skills and company management skills. I was booked in for the tests in Manchester.

I had to do a 1-hour presentation to the general manager of another group. I was given several pages of information of a company in trouble and given 5 hours to restructure to solve the problems. There were also several psychrometric tests. At the end of the second day, the personnel manager took me to a public house to relax and destress me, before I drove home. I eventually received a letter offering me the position.

I had to serve 3 months' notice with Cheshire, before I started my new job in new century house, Manchester, in August 1987.

New team at the Co-op

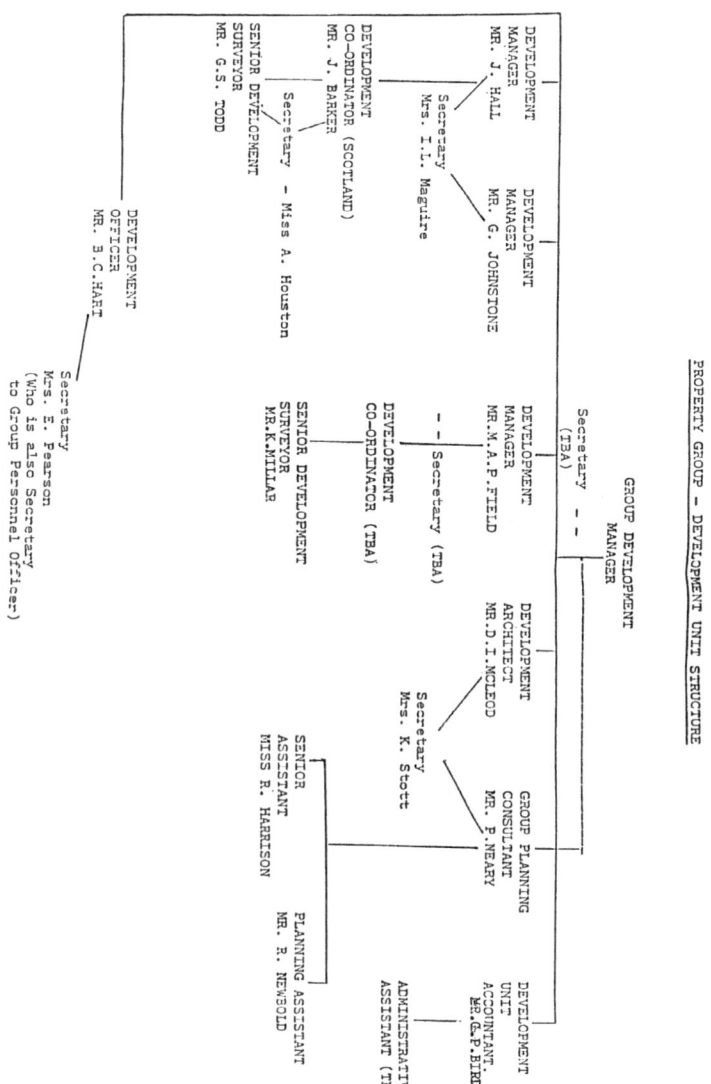

The joint venture companies that existed, when I joined the group, were as follows:

Company Name	**Partner**
Bryco Developments Ltd	Bryants
Crownco Developments Ltd	P&O Properties
Crownco Holdings Ltd	P&O Properties

Crownco Investments Ltd	P&O Properties
Whatco Ltd	Alfred McAlpine
(two boards one for Scotland and one for England)	
Waltham Cross Ltd	Trafalgar House
Shudehill Develpments	CWS, CIS and Maxwell Communications

I was made a director, of all the above companies, except Shudhill Developments Ltd.

Following my employment with CWS, we set up joint ventures, as required, with Ewarts in Northern Ireland, and the Professional Golfers Association European Tour.

Under my control, I had 23 development surveyors, split into 3 teams in Glasgow, Slough and Manchester. Each team had a leader and in Manchester I had two leaders. Several had been colleagues before, including Peter Neary, who had by then obtained a degree in planning and had a small team, specialising in this work.

Brian Hart, who had been my assistant at PDS, was now doing research and checking valuations. Eddie Allan was still head of site assessment and several of his team were still there. John Hall had been Malcolm Clark's assistant at PDS, and he had left to work for a North West developer. He had recently come back to property group when Malcolm had been promoted.

The executive structure of CWS, at that time, was Sir Dennis Landau, as chief executive with two deputies: David Skinner, responsible for retailing group and funerals group, and David Lacey, responsible for everything else, including property group, farms group, engineering group, manufacturing group etc.

In my team, the two leaders were John Hall and George Johnson. John was responsible for Shudehill. This was a proposal to build a major retail shopping scheme in the Shudehill Conservation Area, supported by Manchester City Council. The land required for the development was in the ownership of CWS, CIS and Maxwell Communications.

A joint venture partnership company was negotiated with all three and representatives of each company appointed. John Hall and his assistant Neil Clarke (who was also the company coordinator and wrote the minutes), Rod Burgess from CIS and Derek Shaw, Robert Maxwell's Property man. They formed a good team.

A design team was interviewed and was appointed including Rob Turley as the planning consultant. He had recently left Manchester City Council Planning team to set up his own company. The man, Neil tells me, who was responsible for obtaining the planning consent.

Retail demand had been proven. The shopping gallery, on three levels, would house over 80 shops, a major department store and would have the best car parking facilities in central Manchester. Unfortunately, John was diagnosed with motor neurone disease, shortly after the project had been given planning consent. All of property group, pulled together to raise money to fight this disease, and to provide John with a lift at home.

Two members of the team, Neil Clarke (John's assistant) and Chris Newsome, cycled from Land's End to John O' Groats with 3 stops in Bath, Manchester and Glasgow, to raise money, from all the business contacts we had in each area. Neil and Chris raised £57,000 in total and surprisingly at Derek Shaw's request, Maxwell did donate £5,000 to the blazing saddles charity ride.

When John Hall was unable to carry on working, Neil Clarke became more involved and took greater responsibility. Neil may have been the last person to do a deal with Captain Bob Maxwell, by signing him to commit Maxwell Communications to Shudehill Developments Limited.

Captain Bob was the name he was given by senior staff at CWS, he had been a co-op sponsored Labour MP. This was before he was either pushed or jumped of his yacht. Robert Maxwell's death triggered the collapse of his publishing empire, as banks called in loans.

Maxwell house, a newspaper printing works for the Daily Mirror, was later converted into the Manchester Print Works. It is now a world of entertainment. It is the number one spot in the heart of Manchester for days out with the kids, nights out with your mates and everything in between. The site owners DTZ Investors have recently completed £21 million refurbishment scheme of the leisure centre.

John Whittaker of Peel Holdings had other ideas of what should be built to accommodate the retail demand in Manchester. John Whittaker applied for planning consent for the Trafford Centre, against objections from most of the councils around Manchester, including Manchester City Council. The traffic problems were horrendous, and the battle went on for a long time. Often, the most determined get their way.

Nevertheless, the majority of Mancunians would congratulate Mr Whittaker for his resolve. The Trafford Shopping Centre is a major success, but the amount of traffic is sometimes a problem.

The Trafford Centre killed off the co-op's Shudehill proposed scheme, even though it had received planning consent. The Trafford Centre was in a better location than Shudehill, with a catchment area for the whole of Manchester and beyond, not just the north.

George Johnstone was the property coordinator for Bryco's, the Cranmore Office Park in Solihull, which was a major success for the two partners. Another leader was Lance Field, who I relied on implicitly, for his advice on the most important relationship with P&O and the largest project, the Observatory Shopping Centre in Slough.

In Glasgow, Jonathan Barker had much to do in Northern Ireland and he was also responsible for the development office in Glasgow. His assistant, Graham Todd, did a lot of the Whatco valuations and I used these as a template, for all the other development surveyors in my team.

Noel Cantwell took over from Jonathan when he left, and David Workman took over from Graham Todd when he relocated to the Manchester office. They were both first class commercially aware surveyors. Noel did a difficult job keeping our partnership with Ewarts heading in the right direction.

I was pleased when the Glasgow office closed that he moved to a chief officer post in Aberdeen. Also, David Workman secured a good promotion moving into the private sector.

I encouraged my senior staff to understand planning structure plans and local plans, which were in the planning pipe line, so we could not miss any future opportunities. We did spend a lot of time, with the planning department in Leicester, working on a new settlement to be called Stretton Magna, on our large land holding at Stoughton.

This was our most ambitious project, in terms of scale and quality. It reflected the movement towards privately funded settlements in rural areas, which combine housing with leisure and other facilities.

On the large farm, we had in Down Ampney, in the Cotswolds, we realised that we had a fortune in shale, under the soil. Talking to civil engineers, we discovered that it would be possible to remove the soil, extract the gravel, which would lower the land level and then reinstate the farm soil.

This is easy to say, but without long term commitment, difficult to achieve. We appointed Richard Todd to work with Peter Neary and spend as much time as he needed. This was to build the relationships with the planning authorities, communities and local political groups, with the objective of obtaining planning consent for gravel extraction. Richard made steady progress for the next 20 months, until the Division were instructed to pull out of all joint venture relationships.

Joint Development Companies

Whatco

The Scottish office of property group had set up the first joint venture company, with Whatlings, a builder and developer based in Glasgow. This company had been very successful in refurbishing sandstone tenement blocks, many of which were listed buildings. Whatlings had also been successful in obtaining grants for many of these projects.

The Co-op had many such buildings, in every city throughout Scotland. It was a no brainer that a joint venture company should be set up with Watlings. This company proved that the concept worked, so why not do the same in England? Malcolm's relationship with one of the partners of Alfred McAlpine, David Deas, was in many ways, very beneficial for property group. This led to McAlpine's taking over Whatlings. David also introduced the Professional Golfers Association European Tour to property group.

The joint venture with the European Tour was to build the main tournament golf course venues for the next century. There was no shortage of land for this venture from CWS farms group.

Farms group professed to be the largest farmer in Europe, farming the land direct, not letting the land onto farmers, and they also had the largest milk quota.

One farm was located in Cheshire, at Weston Hall, near Crewe. I had dealt with the Chief Executive of Crewe & Nantwich Borough Council, over the Crewe Business Park, so I made an appointment to meet him. I said there was an opportunity to put Crewe on the map, in golfing terms, but I would need his help!

It would be good if he could assign one of his senior planning officers to be part of our development team, to work on the planning application. I also appointed an architect in Chester, Philip McCormick, to design the houses, working with the retired head of planning from Warrington New Town.

There was also assigned to the team, Richard Hill, from the PGA. Richard organised for the team of 8 to go to America, to visit the top PGA courses in Florida, Texas and Chicago. I also included Neil Clarke to be involved as the work expanded and the Shudehill scheme was not then taking all his time.

A design team of experts in landscaping, planning, quantity surveying, architectural matters and golf course design, set off for the USA. The Americans at the PGA courses were lavish in providing information on, golf course design, house design and layout briefs to their architects.

They also provided legal documents on how strictly they controlled the residents of the houses so there was no conflict with tournament golf. When I left CWS, I left this information behind. However, Neil Clarke had some photographs which I will copy below.

We started in Miami, Florida and visited several courses before going to Houston in Texas. We then went to Pensacola to visit Seaside, at the base of the panhandle, one of the first communities in America designed on the principles of New Urbanism.

It was ridiculously hot. I remember seeing a lot of golf courses including Eagle Trace and Tournament Players Course at the Woodlands. We visited more which I cannot remember.

It was an ambitious program with a lot of driving and a test of our stamina. We were a mixed bunch, spread over two cars, it was hardly easy rider as we had a succession of hire cars with unfamiliar controls. I remember one member of the team wanting to do most of the driving.

Maybe he was unfamiliar with the auto transmission and electric brakes, but I remember that at one stage we were driving on the highway at high speed, and he was complaining that the car was underpowered and not pulling properly. After a while, there was a smell of burning and he had to pull over.

We all piled out and found that he had been driving with the brakes partly on. As a result, the brake discs on the car were glowing red hot, literally red hot, and it took a long time to let them cool down completely.

Everyone seemed to get on well enough. Barry and Phil were especially good company, some a bit pompous, Sue fitted in well and could hold her own as the sole woman, not surprising, as she had a landscape design company. One member of the group was forever losing things.

It was papers and mostly articles of clothing. It was shoes and definitely a jacket. We stayed in different hotels, nearly every night, a lot of packing and unpacking, so if they were sent on they would never catch up.

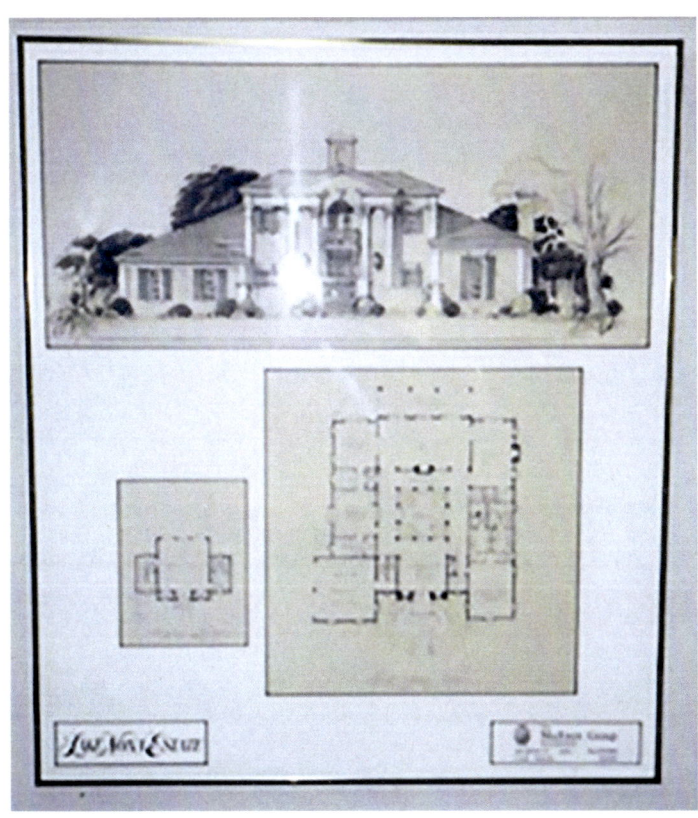

 Neil and I said good bye to the design team when they went back to Manchester and we flew to Chicago, Illinois to visit Kemper Lakes. Another PGA golf course. We were treated by this golf course with the same excellent hospitality as the ones in Florida. Neil and I had other reasons to visit Chicago.

Neil was working on finding the right architect for the Shudehill scheme and we wanted to visit the main major shopping centre in Chicago. He had identified Kohn Pederson Fox, who had designed 333 Wacker Drive in Chicago. Neil had already had conversations with the company on how their work would relate to downtown Manchester.

I will always remember our last day in Chicago. Neil and I had just left the large shopping centre we had come to see, when the heavens opened with driving rain and a gale force wind. I instinctively open my umbrella and the wind blew it inside out. Neil instinctively took the photo of me in the windy city, which sums up the trip.

At Western Hall, Crewe Borough Council eventually granted a detailed planning consent for 725 acres of land, comprising a tournament course, club course, 500 fairway homes, hotel and other leisure facilities. Not long after the planning application had been given a consent, a few local residents, in Crewe objected to the route of the Barthomley link road and submitted an alternative proposal.

This went through part of the planned golf course. We knew that this problem would take a long time to resolve, so we built the first phase of the spine road, to secure the detailed planning consent. We then packed up on site, until it was resolved. By then, I had left CWS. The development with consent was sold to another residential developer, so the PGA never had tournament golf in Crewe.

Go-ahead for top golf course

Crewe Chronicle 14 May 90

THE GO-AHEAD has been given for one of the top golf courses in Europe to be built near Crewe.

The Government's green light for the £50m complex will bring two 18-hole courses, 500 swish new homes, a luxury hotel and golf academy to Weston.

With them will come the world's top golfers and world-wide TV and media coverage.

News that Environment Secretary Nicholas Ridley has decided not to intervene in the plan to develop the 725 site at Weston Hall was announced on Monday.

Plans for the country's first purpose-built golf stadium, which puts a premium on spectator accommodation, were first discussed in January 1988.

Crewe and Nantwich Borough Council, despite strong opposition from local residents, finally gave planning approval in March last year.

Since then a decision has been awaited from the Environment Secretary who called it in for special consideration because it strayed from Cheshire County Council's structure plan.

The scheme is a joint venture between the CWS who own the land; Whatco, a joint company owned by the CWS and Alfred McAlpine, and the Professional

Weston

Golfers' Association European Tour.

Work will begin immediately on producing a detailed scheme and actual groundwork is expected to follow later this year.

Former Ryder Cup player Neil Coles, now executive chairman of the PGA European Tour Properties, delighted with the news, commented: 'This is good news for golf and a major step forward for the development of the sport in Britain.

'Weston Hall will be a golf complex, designed not just for players, but for spectators, who will be accommodated in a way never before built into UK golf courses.'

By Alan Jervis

'This is the first spectator course designed and built to major tournament standards, as defined by the PGA European Tour.'

And Richard Hills, the PGA European Tour Properties managing director, added: 'This is the first of what I term the new generation of golf courses. We often hear that new championship courses are to be built, but this one really is a championship course in the truest sense.'

Mr Hills said if everything went according to plan, golf would first be played on the two courses by late 1992 or early 1993. He expected the first PGA Tour events to come to Weston by 1995 or '96.

The Championship 'South Course' will measure 7,324 yards according to the original plans, and the North Course, for members and guests will be only, a little shorter at 6,910 yards. Both will have a par of 72, the Championship course having four par fives, three of them measuring 500 yards or more.

Although the news will be welcomed by the golfing and sporting fraternity in general, the scheme has its opposition too.

Several hundred local people signed a petition of protest against the idea originally, claiming it would ruin the area — changing it into a 'Yuppie village'.

And on Monday, Mr Bert Latham, chairman of the governors of Weston School, said: 'I believe it will bring a nightmare to the area. But although the Environment Secretary called it in, we never really doubted that he would give it the go-ahead.

'A piece of land on the site has been designated for a new school, but no-one has ever said that we are definitely going to get the school. And I dread to think of youngsters mingling with all that additional traffic.

'But I suppose all we can do now is monitor the scheme as closely as we can and see that the developers don't step out of line.'

Housing estates all over England and Scotland were developed when Whatco moved to McAlpine's Head Office near Chester. A very profitable situation for both the CWS and McAlpine's.

CrownCo

CROWNGAP banked with the Co-operative bank and found itself in a financial situation, that had got too big for it to fail. This was the reason why property group was feeding very profitable developments into this joint company. Large office blocks had been developed and sold, and planning consent had been granted, to build a shopping centre in Slough.

This was too big for CROWNGAP, so along came P&O Developments, to purchase CROWNGAP. P&O was, and is, a strong company, with many strands to its empire. Bovis was one of its subsidiaries. The shopping centre was built and named the Observatory.

Bryco

Bryants Head Office, in Solihull, overlooked a large Co-op site, which had been declared surplus to requirements. Planning consent was obtained for the Cranmore Business Park, so who better to form a joint company with, than Bryants. This was a very successful and profitable development.

Waltham Cross Developments

The Co-op owned a large site with access onto the M25 at Waltham Cross. We thought that, with Trafalgar House, as the joint venture partner, we would have credibility and have a good chance of success. We applied for planning consent for a business park of 500,000 sq. ft of B1 space, and if granted, they would act as developer.

However, the site was in the Green Belt and planning would take some considerable time. At the Waltham Cross board meeting on 17 March 1993, Rex Mercer of Drivers Jonas, thought that Broxbourne Borough Council, together with Trafalgar House support, the Inspector would support the application. This would possibly be subject to certain conditions, to ensure that the site was used for Policy 74 purposes, (special technological uses or uses in the national or regional interest).

BOARD REPORT

WALTHAM CROSS

On 15th June 1988 CWS entered into an Option Agreement with **Waltham Cross Developments** (a joint company between CWS and Trafalgar House) for the Society's land at Waltham Cross on the following terms:

Consideration for Option	:	£10 000
Option period	:	4 years
Exercise of Option	:	Any time after grant of planning permission
Initial Consideration (payable upon exercise of Option)	:	£12 483 900
Developers profit @ 20% on costs of development	:	to be split 50/50 between CWS/Trafalgar House
'Development Super Profit' (i.e. in excess of aggregate of Initial Consideration and developers profit)	:	to be split 65/35 between CWS/Trafalgar House
Development Loss	:	not explicit; <u>assumed</u> to be split 50/50 between CWS/Trafalgar House but without recourse to Initial Consideration

The above Option Agreement expired on the 4th June 1992

It is now proposed to enter into a new Option Agreement on the following terms:

Consideration for Option	:	£10 000
Option Period	:	until 14th June 2002 or three years from grant of planning permission whichever earlier
Exercise of Option	:	any time after grant of planning permission
Initial Consideration (payable upon exercise of of option subject to agreement between parties but no later than 3 years from exercise)	:	based on a residual land valuation (no minimum sum) gain over agricultural land value and split 75/25 between CWS/Trafalgar House

Developers profit @ 20% on costs of development (First Call)	:	split 50/50 between CWS/Trafalgar House (land value element to be fixed for this calculation at Initial Consideration value)

Upon completion of development

In event of 'development Super Profit'	:	
Second Call profit	:	determined at a maximum 20% of Initial Consideration and split 75/25 between CWS/Trafalgar House
Third Call profit (balance)	:	to be split 50/50 between CWS/Trafalgar House
In event of development loss	:	
First charge shortfall	:	determined at a maximum 20% of Initial Consideration and split 75/25 between CWS/Trafalgar House
Second charge shortfall (balance)	:	to be split 50/50 between CWS/Trafalgar House

May we please have authority to enter into an Option Agreement with Waltham Cross Developments on the above terms.

However, there's many a slip twixt the cup and the lip.

Trafalgar house, also owned several hotels in London, including the Ritz. Is there any better place to hold a board meeting?

Joint Ventures

The Northern Ireland Cooperative Society was no longer viable, so it was either pull out and not trade in the province, or build bigger retail units, preferably in shopping centres.

A meeting in Malcolm's office was arranged to discuss the purchase of the Gallagher Tobacco Factory, in the New Lodge Estate, about 1 mile east of Belfast City Centre. One of the men invited was John McElroy, the MD of Ewarts, a Property

Development Company and John McLennan, who was freelance and had worked in a top position, in the Civil Service.

Jonathan Barker, the leader of my Glasgow team, had been across to Northern Island, scouting for superstore sites. I went with Jonathan to Belfast, and we toured the city and visited the tobacco factory, on a 13 acres site. The multi-storey buildings had been constructed by Alfred McAlpine, with a specification to take very heavy tobacco machinery; it would last for ever.

We noticed, whilst driving around the New Lodge Estate, that British soldiers were in units of four, with machine guns on alert. The New Lodge Estate was a no go area for the troops at that time. It was obvious that we would need a local joint venture partner, in the province, with a track record in retail development.

Ewarts was a company, which had been in the linen manufacturing industry and evolved into property development, so they became our partner. Town centre schemes in Ballymena, (this one anchored by M&S) and Bangor, were successfully developed.

British Council of Shopping Centres Conference in Bournemouth

Dinner in Manchester

The End Game at CWS

In 1991, Malcolm moved from Frodsham to Doncaster. I was puzzled by this move! The job entailed a lot of driving, and you would not want to increase this, unless you had to, for family reasons. He was then rarely seen in the office, unless he had a meeting with David Lacey, the deputy chief executive. At this time, it was approaching Sir Dennis Landau's retirement and there was a lot of speculation about who would be appointed. Would it be one of the two deputies Lacey or Skinner?

Malcolm did not stay around to find out. On a Friday night, he resigned form CWS, leaving everyone flummoxed. The following week, Steven Redfern came into my office with the news that a planning application had been submitted, to Doncaster Council, for a major development, to include a business park, a large housing estate and golf course.

It was obvious that Malcolm was involved in this proposal. I had known Malcolm long enough, to know that he would use the political approach, which is acceptable as long as there is planning support. I recognised the consultants involved, as we had been using them for a long time.

It had been obvious to Malcolm, that if Skinner was appointed, it would be the end of property group, as he knew it. Malcolm proved to be correct in this assumption.

Malcolm had insisted that, out of my budget, I paid for two political advisors. I had a good relationship with them both, but I would not have employed them.

On performance, I thought Skinner had no chance. Co-op retailing was then extremely poor. I had attended a British Council of Shopping Centres Conference. After the Chief Executive of Kingfisher, John Mulcahy, had explained how the company had moved from the old Woolworths days to the days of B&Q, I asked him what significant change of policy helped the company move forward.

He said introducing, in the accounts, charging each store the open market rent. This indicated the good from the bad. I subsequently put this information in a number of reports and challenged the head of Co-op retailing at a Co-op property conference, with this information.

At this time, CWS was desperate for finance, as the burden of supporting many failed retail societies, had become critical. This Mulcahy solution was rejected. I had been asked to sell a hypermarket in the South East of England. I was told that what Tesco had offered, was unbelievable, but it would be like the Queen selling Buckingham Palace.

Nevertheless, Mr Skinner was appointed chief executive.

Looking back, at the age of 80, I do have some sympathy for Co-op retailing at that time. It was difficult for the Co-op to compete with the operations of say Tesco or Asda, as the majority of retailing was still under the control of individual retail societies.

Today Co-op retailing is very successful, and they are able to compete on what they do best. The small local, late night, Co-op shops, operating on a national basis, with a membership discount cards and contributions to community schemes, has proved to be very good business. The modern replacement of the old Co-op dividend.

This transformation was achieved in 2000 by the merger of CWS and Co-op Retail Services, to form the Co-op group. This was followed in 2007 by the merger of United Cooperatives with the Co-op group. In 2009, the Co-op Food business acquired Somerfield's, a rival business, and in 2018 it acquired Nisa, enabling Co-op own brand range to be stocked in Nisa convenience stores.

Today Co-op group is the UK's largest mutual business, owned by millions of UK consumers.

Co-op Retailing Takes Over

I had a meeting with Peter Neary and his team, in about 1990, when the joint companies and the development programme, was looking its best. I thought we had a product, in planning and development terms, which could be successful, in the open market. A brochure was produced, and I think it would have produced good results for the group and CWS.

After Malcolm resigned, David Lacey appointed Ron Dixon, as general manager of property group. He had been David Lacey's right hand man for many years. A very clever accountant, who you would want on your side, in any joint company operation.

I learned a lot from Ron, in the limited time we were colleagues. Ron restructured property group, along the lines of asset management, with many staff leaving. I thought the slimmed down property group was the right vehicle for the future.

Nevertheless, all work on development and joint company operations had been stopped. I was instructed to rewind from the joint company business. In June 1992, the group was restructured to reflect the state of the property market and the needs of the society.

In my new position, under Ron, I was responsible for a team of asset managers, based solely in Manchester. The portfolio comprised 800 properties, in England and Scotland, with a rent roll of £16m and a market value in excess of £160m. The overriding instruction was to sell as the society needed capital.

Ron was made redundant along with many more members of property group. I held my job, for the time being, as I was still extracting the CWS from the joint company operations. I knew that if Ron Dixon was no longer required, decisions were being made for political reasons and it was nothing to do with ability.

The post of general manager of the group was advertised, and I applied for the position. I was interviewed by Mr Skinner's, Head of Personnel, who smoked a pipe throughout the interview, at the same time tearing strips off my application form, to relight his pipe. I didn't need a letter of rejection.

My new boss was Bob Galley (ex. Prudential), who had been recruited from the residuary body of Manchester City Council, having dealt with their superannuation fund. This was a similar role to the one I had at Cheshire. Bob and I may have been able to work together, but it was clear that he had been briefed that anyone involved in the success of David Lacey's time, was no longer required.

Redundancy

I was made redundant in January 1994. I was given 2 weeks to decide if I wanted to take my pension now and lose 40% of the value, or leave it invested and take it when I eventually retired. I had never been made redundant before and thought I may not obtain another job, so to my later regret, I opted to take my pension then.

The most important concern is how this event affected my mentality. I have throughout most of my life had a mantra, that I would write in my diary. The diary was mainly a list of where I had to be at a certain time, so it was checked every day. On leaving school, my mantra was simple, you're only as good as you think you are.

The shock of redundancy took much more psychological analysis. I needed a new mantra that I could build up my confidence on. It took me several weeks to come to terms with how I felt. Eventually, I knew I felt disillusioned, so it was only the loss of an illusion. I wrote this in my diary.

I have no complaints over my leaving package, it allowed me to keep my company car for 6 months, although they did try to wriggle out of the pension agreement, that Ron Dixon had secured some time before.

The leaving package with KPMG, included secretarial support, lectures and the use of their computers. They hoped to find me an equivalent role, with another company. I taught myself to type and I did attend several lectures.

However, I decided to work for myself, as a property development consultant, and KPMG designed my business card and letter heading. I then secured a consultancy with NatWest Bank, to do a property audit, prior to their computerising their property portfolio.

The audit was being carried out across the UK by DTZ (Bernard Thorpe & Partners), except for the North West, where George Perrin was in charge. It was a two-man job, for a solicitor and a chartered surveyor. Mr David Nixon was the solicitor, who arrived 2 weeks after me. We were friends from the start. David was a member at Lords, and entertained George and me there, on a number of occasions. It was always a special treat.

The job, we thought, *would last for about 6 to 8 months.* After I had been at NatWest for a few months, I saw the chief estate surveyor's post at Ellesmere Port & Neston, advertised. I applied and was offered the post. I knew the authority well, as I had done many projects in the Borough, over the 11 years that I had worked for Cheshire. George Perrin was reasonable but insisted that I had contracted to do the job, and it was up to me to find a replacement.

I knew who to appoint, someone academically able and available to take my place, but who might cause friction with colleagues, especially women. I explained all this to David Nixon, and he thought there would be no problems now that he had been forewarned. The man I recommended completed the assignment with David. They had a common interest in music and visited the Halle many times. Nevertheless, the office girls refused to bring the individual, the required property files, and David had to resolve the situation.

Ellesmere Port and Neston Borough Council

My final salary when I left the CWS in January 1994, as group asset manager, was £56,626, plus top of the range company car and generous expenses. My new salary as chief estates surveyor, with the council was £24,636 (plus my CWS pension) with no obvious perks. One advantage was that it was not far to drive, from my home in Chester to Ellesmere Port.

Also, the job covered all aspects of property work, valuation, development and estate management. My family and social life should significantly improve. The job also gave me a new challenge, the management of two markets. I was 51, and I wanted to enjoy the last 10 years of my career.

The one area I had not thought about, was attending committees, which were always in the evening, starting at 7:00 pm and often lasting to10:00 pm. I never had to attend any evening committee meetings at Cheshire County Council.

I had a good relationship with all the labour councillors, and many became friends. Di Davies who visited my office, at least once a week, was the councillor who was most involved with the market. Councillor Crimes, who chaired the finance committee, also became a friend.

At budget time, he would have a day with me, going through

the property portfolio to extract every penny. I involved Teresa McGroarty in this exercise; she was pragmatic and could find opportunities to satisfy his requirements. The majority of the industrial units were less than 2,000 sq. ft and did not have long leases, which enabled more opportunities to increase rent.

The relationship with councillors was totally different working for a district council. Members would walk into my office, at any time of day, or knock on my window (being on the ground floor) for a discussion about some local problem.

The post of chief estates surveyor came under the Borough Solicitor, Jim Bickerton, who reported to the Chief Executive and Town Clerk, Stephen Ewbank. Jim was not happy about a recent restructuring of the council, that had given him responsibility for property, and which had also demoted him from the council's management board. This was eventually rectified by my reporting to the Chief Executive and Town Clerk and Jim becoming Borough Solicitor and central services officer, but still not on the management board.

Once I had got to know the individuals in my team, I introduced a new office structure. as set out below:

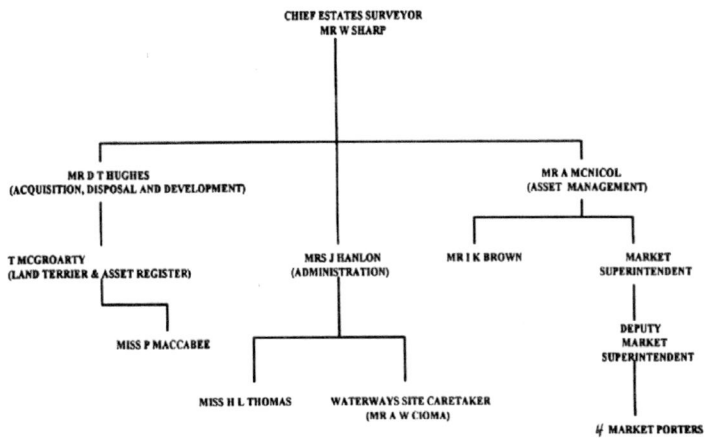

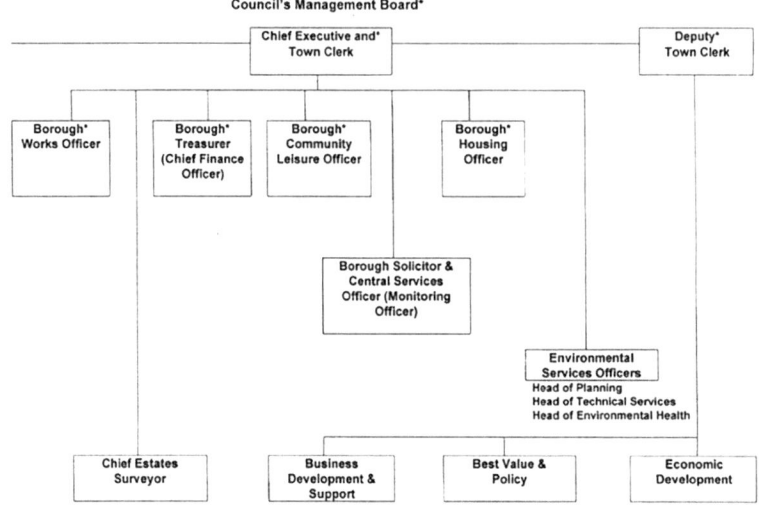

In July 1994, the team were managing the following property holdings:

1. 7 industrial estates with 191 units
2. 6 retail parades with 49 lock-up shops
3. Ellesmere Port and Neston markets comprising 220 stalls (and 60 lock-up units in the EP market)
4. 94 ground leases, including Ellesmere Port town centre and Neston town centre.
5. 79 miscellaneous properties
6. 15 available development sites totalling 80 acres, mainly for industrial development.
7. Greyhound Racing Stadium

The income for this 12 months' period was £1.6 million. The industrial units were all over 90% let, with hardly any voids. This reflected the strong demand for small industrial units of less than 2000 sq. ft.

Rental Income Stream Comparison

Code	Description	Actual 1993/1994 £	Actual 1999/2000 £		
B021	EP Town Centre	209370	246829		
B031	Property Acquired	2864			
B041	Garages	4724	5658		
B051	Carnegie	3060	6318		
B061	Canalside	8614	17000		
B070	Clayhill	129155	181441		
B081	Coronation	15030	19818		
B085	Craft Workshops	25647	25008		
B090	Meadow/Crescent	9100	16952		
B091	Meadow Lane Ind Estate	76542	86685		
B101	Merseyton	103269	106055		
B131	Poole Hall	97628	112619		
B135	Portside	13500	13500		
B141	Rossmore Estate	44185	30288		
B142	Rossmore Terraced Factories	44620	58063		
B151	Shrewsbury	12687	10356		
B161	Stanney Mill	65299	93223		
B171	Thornton	10774	13965		
B181	Westminster	101609	122734		
B191	Whitby Rd	10601	8276		
B302	Whitby Lodge		16000		
B303/B306	Neston Town Hall	12555	9475		
M001	EP Market	569258	735680		
M002	Neston Market	44513	44817		
H001	Commercial premises HRA	83920	94696		
TOTAL		**£1,698,524**	**£2,075,456**	22%	increase

The above figures do not reflect property disposals (e.g. McCormicks) which have produced capital to the detriment of the income stream.

The estates team had not been well managed for some considerable time, and I was welcomed. The next 10 years were a busy time and we achieved a great deal for the council.

On my first day at Ellesmere Port, I asked my team if there were any problems that needed attention? Alisdair said he had two, both relating to Ellesmere Port Market. The flea market manager responsible for the Sunday and Thursday second hand markets was in breach of his contract terms.

This was being dealt with the following week at an arranged meeting. There was a list of work, he was contracted to do, that he did not do. Handing over a clean market on a Monday morning was the most costly and difficult to deal with. This meant the market porters had to do the work, which was not in their job specification.

Also, there was a list of items he was not allowed to sell, which he allowed the traders to sell. I asked Alisdair what he recommended. He thought that we should terminate his contract. Alisdair had costed out a scheme which showed that the council could run both of these markets, at a higher profit. The other item concerned the manager of the Council's market, Bill Stewart. I did not consider this to be urgent as it would take some time to resolve.

When the meeting took place with the second-hand market manager, I told him that we were not renewing his contract and I explained why.

On the following Wednesday, I was in Neston with Ian Brown, getting to know the council's property in the Neston area. I was requested to come back to the office, as Fred Venables, Leader of the Council, wished to see me in Jim Bickerton's office.

I arrived back and Fred wanted to know why I was not prepared to renew this manager's contract. I repeated all that Alisdair had told me, which indicated that he may be being subsidised by the council to operate an asset which they already owned. I was told to report my view to the appropriate committee.

I was not surprised that the committee did not terminate his whole contract, because markets were very popular for the sale of second-hand tools, books, videos, and clothes, but they did terminate his contract on the Thursday market. We then took the management of the Thursday market in house but not as a second-hand market.

Alisdair represented the department on the market traders' liaison committee, chaired by councillor Di Davis and the traders were represented by Keith Tickle (a shoe trader). This committee sorted out most of the problems, but not all. A small number of market traders did not like each other. One morning one trader head butted another, and the market superintendent requested that I deal with the matter.

It was important that management did not take sides and dealt with any violence quickly. I took my lead from rugby referees by remaining unbiased and retaining credibility. I arranged to meet each of the traders separately on a one-to-one basis, telling each that they were banned from trading until I had investigated.

Di Davis did not want to be involved and trusted me to sort it out quickly, which I did. This was fairly easy to do as there were no secrets in the market and such events would have been festering for some time.

Bill Stewart (previous market superintendent) was given early retirement, and a redundancy settlement was paid. Alisdair and I were determined that the new market manager would be appointed in a best practice way. We had prepared several questions to ask, to be able to decide who had performed the best, which the labour councillors approved.

The meeting commenced and then Brenda Dowding, a Conservative councillor from Neston, arrived. I quickly explained what we had agreed to be the format for the interview. She responded that she would ask whatever she wanted and would not be taking any advice from me! Nevertheless, we all agreed that the best candidate was Alan Jones, and he was appointed. Later we appointed an assistant to Alan, called Gerry, to cover the management role.

Market Superintendent with the Mayor

Eventually the second-hand manager retired and as there was a general view that Sunday should be operated by an outside operator and the market porters should not be made to work on Sundays. The Sunday market was put out to competition.

The winner of the competition was Tuebrook Motor Auctions, who ran a market on their site at the former Tuebrook Station Goods Yard. The main man was PJ Doherty known to one and all as PJ. He was a personable Irishman who got on with everyone.

The achievements the team made, included the improvement of the town centre retail centre, Port Arcades, which was on long lease from the council. The problem was mainly that a lot of the zone A shopping space was in circulation space and not let for retailing. It was possible to accommodate larger units with better covenants, improve the centre and eventually the council's ground rent. This had to be dealt with tactfully. Consultants were appointed to bring this to the owners' attention, for the centre was quite a new development.

The development of the first phase of Cheshire Oaks had commenced before I started work at the council. I knew the site well as I had been involved with Cheshire Highways to have a bull head access slip, on the roundabout at junction 10 on the M53, because of the land's potential. I had also developed a small industrial site, Stanney Ten, linking into the same roundabout.

Rob McKenzie in the planning department was supporting Stephen Ewbank, in this project and they were doing an excellent job. The chief planning officer, Tom Miller should be praised for the excellent landscaping on the development.

The only involvement my team had was pointing out to Stephen Ewbank, the large planning gain opportunity for the council. I believe that Stephen Ewbank should have received a Knighthood for the development of Cheshire Oaks, which may not have happened without him.

The catchment area for Cheshire Oaks covers most of the North West and North Wales, visitors often remark about how few empty shop units there are. This could be because they are on a turnover rent basis.

The Borough Council had 80 acres of vacant industrial development land with good access to the M53 motorway. Brenda Harvey the Economic Development Officer, at that time, pointed out that we could obtain grant support to help market this land.

We set up a team to interview several North West agents, to appoint one to give this advice. Brian Birtwistle was appointed and reported back on a regular basis.

The council also had let land to many companies, on a long lease basis with a very tight user clause. I used this clause, when the occupier vacated, to secure a high land value, for the release of said covenant. Agents acting for buyers often objected to what I was asking, in one case one of the Liverpool agents made this a major issue, in relation to Ashfield Hall Farm, in Neston.

I had been involved in this development when I was working for the County Council, at the invitation of Mr R J Bernie OBE, LLB, the then Chief Executive of EP&NBC. I was aware of the user clause and Stephen Ewbank backed my judgment.

The Liverpool agent pulled out of the deal for the leisure development on the basis I was asking too much. I then sold the long leasehold interest to one of the German retailers for the development of a regional warehouse, at my asking price. It was a pleasure to deal with this company, they build to a high standard and the landscaping was excellent.

The largest single income producer, by far, was Ellesmere Port Market. I had to obtain management board's approval for any unbudgeted expenditure; I often found myself frustrated by their lack of interest.

Nevertheless, although I was not a chief officer, I was not surprised, when best value review came along, to find that I was responsible for leading a team of 5 councillors, to do a review of all my council responsibilities. This included Ellesmere Port Market. Although it was a big income producer, it was past it's sell by date in many ways.

It did not meet modern day hygiene standards, on the sale of food and meat. The 140 pitches had to be erected each day, with traders driving into the market hall, to set up their stalls. The fumes from poorly maintained vehicles also caused health problems. It was not possible to keep the birds out, even with providing plastic birds of prey. Bird droppings were also a problem.

The review was, not only to look at the market as it was, but also the plans for improvement of the service. Much to the surprise of management board, the market got a good review, based on the plans for improvement.

My boss, Stephen Ewbank, started to take an interest. Asda, the owner of the main anchor of the town centre, was invited into the office to discuss their superstore and what could be achieved, with the added value, created by a new development of a hypermarket for Asda and relocating the market traders into their existing superstore.

The objective was that all the costs, including the relocation of all the market traders, would be met by Asda. This meeting started the negotiations that led to relocating the market into a modern market building.

Jane Williamson the Borough's architect and I did a lot of work to make this happen. The most important role for me, was to ensure the council met the legal requirements on achieving best value, under the local government acts. It did not help that the new Borough Solicitor refused to be involved and I had to obtain legal advice from a firm of private practice solicitors.

I had to negotiate with all the market traders, to secure vacant possession, to enable the development to start. The heads of terms of the deal was finally negotiated in the Manchester office of Eversheads, Asda's Manchester solicitors, on 17 June 2004.

I picked up Graham Keating in Frodsham to take him with me to the meeting which concluded at about 8pm, after working through lunch. I had appointed Graham after Alisdair McNicol (a big loss to me) had left to join Wirral Borough Council. I thought Graham was a commercially competent surveyor, who with David Hughes, would retain and strengthen the existing team.

The meeting had exhausted me, and I drove home with a pain

L to R.—Alisdair McNicol, Me, David Hughes, Ian Brown

at the top of my arm; my wife had to telephone for a paramedic at 1:45 am, which led to my leaving Ellesmere Port several months later. The paramedic told me that in future I should take my doctor's advice.

In 2003, I had been suffering from angina when I went to the gym, on the way to work. This resulted in my having an angiogram at Arrow Park hospital, on the Wirral, on 26 June 2003. The consultant explained that I had a blocked artery, which was too far advanced to have a stent fitted.

I was put on a number of pills to reduce my cholesterol and to deal with high blood pressure etc. My doctor strongly advised that I should only work part time to reduce stress. I ignored this advice and went back to work full time on 17 July 2003.

I eventually took his advice, lost weight and improved my fitness by joining the Chester hill walking and rambling club. The club had been founded in 1919, one of the first in the UK.

Like most estates departments in the UK, my team had to deal with gypsies trespassing on Borough land. The police if requested were required to support my team on site when we had to serve notice on each caravan. They often did not turn up. It often became a hostile environment.

I had done reports to management board about the issue, to no avail, even suggesting that other departments were better able to deal with this issue. After Ian Brown had been knocked to the ground and attacked by dogs (but not bitten), I requested that the trade union handle the matter with management board. I then was able to appoint Bailiffs as contractors to deal with the gypsies.

Looking at my time at CCC and at Ellesmere Port, the big political difference was that the county put a lot of time and money into ensuring that democracy prevailed. It was important that all political parties were treated the same. At the county, under Sir John Boynton, a lot more responsibility was delegated to senior staff.

They were trusted to look after the county's interests. At Ellesmere Port, there was a Monday morning meeting with the Leader of the Council, Fred Venables and his deputy, Reg Chrimes. I had to make myself available on Monday mornings, often I was up and down like a shuttlecock.

Decisions were made on all the important issues which were then voted on at committee. The Labour party had a major majority so what had been agreed on the Monday morning, was always carried. It would not have made any difference to the end result, but I think this is worth recording.

Unfortunately, my doctor was steadfast in not allowing me to work full time and management board were steadfast in not allowing this to happen. This stand-off lasted several months.

I then had a message from Pam Williams, Borough Treasurer, to say that management board had agreed that I could come back part time and the chief executive would share my work load. Good news. I agreed to the proposal, but required, how it would work in writing. The letter never came. Several months later I was allowed to retire.

This situation could have been easily resolved. I would have come back part time under Pam Williams.

I enjoyed my 10 years at Ellesmere Port and Neston and at 62 was ready for retirement.

ACES

ACES is the acronym of the Association of Chief Estate Surveyors and property managers in the local government. Most professions within local government have an organisation dedicated to their respective concerns and ACES is the one for local authority property professionals.

The authoritative status as ACES is recognised by the bodies that are involved in the formulation of polices which affect local authorities property activities. It has formal consultation links with the department of the environment, the Royal Institution of chartered surveyors, the chief valuer of the Inland Revenue and the local government association. It is also in regular contact with organisations representing other professional disciplines within local government.

There has been an increasing awareness of the enormous property assets held by local authorities and the need for effective management of these substantial investments. A consequence is that property professionals now have to operate in an environment which is subject to frequent changes, which often have a far reaching affect.

ACES aims not only to ensure that its members are kept informed of changes which will affect their daily work but also seeks to ensure that there is balanced professional input into new proposals.

In my opinion, the most important role for a senior property man, in the public sector is the custodian of the property portfolio. This includes ensuring that open market value is obtained in any disposal. This is a legal requirement and gives power to your elbow, if you have a chief officer or councillor who likes to dabble in property.

I have prided myself in having a clean record in this regard. Section 123 of the Local Government Act spells this out, it gives you many options, but it is wise to be able to prove that you have received best value. In my job at Cheshire and Ellesmere Port, property was always advertised, and development opportunities were always put out to tender.

If in any doubt, have an independent RICS surveyor to value and write a letter confirming that best value has been achieved. I had to do this a number of times, such as the deal with ASDA for the relocation of E.P. market. The senior partner of one of the Manchester firms wrote such a report.

Valuation surveyors should never underestimate the importance of residual valuations. It makes you the most important member of any development team and to speak candidly the team should be led by you. All the ingredients in the valuation enable you to assess viability and know were any problem lies.

ACES also produces a high-quality journal, The Terrier, published quarterly and a year book, Per Annum which gives details of its officers, branches, working groups, individual members and member authorities.

Although I had been involved with this association, whilst at Cheshire County Council, as it organised the courses and lectures for professional staff to help maintain their continuous professional development requirement, at modest cost. I was not the chief officer and not allowed to join. My new team at Ellesmere Port insisted that I join, as soon as possible, so they could benefit professionally, and they knew it would be good for networking.

I not only joined but was voted on to the North West committee and became Chairman in the year 2000.

When I was with ERS&K, James Rushton had asked me to join the junior branch of the incorporated society of valuers & auctioneers, saying it would be good for me and good for ERS&K. I did join and soon had a lot of friends in this professional body. My best man, Rodney Barlow and I met at my first society meeting in the Midland hotel in Manchester.

I had to walk around the block several times summoning up the courage to go in. I was involved, for many years, in organising the annual Turkey Supper, I bought the raffle presents and booked one of the best comedians in Manchester, at that time. It was always a sell-out. We had the Turkey Supper in the restaurant, owned by Salford City Council, in Langworthy Park.

ACES enabled local authorities to better compete with the private sector. A private company had received authority to lay cables in the roads around Ellesmere Port. Through ACES, I soon discovered which authorities the company had already visited and the details of their deal.

When I worked for Ellesmere Port & Neston, I knew most of the chief estate surveyors in the North West, through my connections and involvement in ACES. Amalgamation of professional property bodies, eventually led to us all becoming chartered surveyors. I was made a fellow of the RICS in January 2000.

One of the most important ingredients in becoming a successful property man is being able to network.

Buy to Let

Rodney Barlow and I decided in the early 1970s to buy property to let, as we were both in the property business. He was working for an estate agent in Salford, and I worked for Salford City Council. I would not start to do this with Rodney, until I left Salford in 1972 and moved to Peterborough.

We both knew that buying houses under the old Housing Acts and the rent officer controlling the level of rent, would significantly reduce the market value. We had a very successful hobby, buying and selling houses for the next 27 years, until I bought my last property, an apartment in Chester, in 1999. We both put our careers and family first, and often did not do for this for several years at a time, as other events took priority.

When riots were taking place in Moss Side, Manchester, three of us acquired 6 houses in Moss Side, with a loan from a bank. The weakness in doing this was that the rent officer never increased the rent, to the market level, so when we obtained vacant possession, we sold and looked for the next purchase. I have recently put my last property, an apartment in Chester on the market to sell. Rodney died in 2023.

I must pay tribute to the labour administration of Salford City Council who introduced for landlords a licencing scheme. I was one of the first landlords, possibly the first, to join this scheme. I have a photograph of me in the front of my property in Liverpool Street that appeared in the local paper to advertise the scheme.

It was a case of carrot or stick. If you were a licenced landlord, you had to comply with the council's standards on the condition of the property, how you managed the property and fire safety requirements et cetera. If you did not become a licenced landlord and meet the council's requirements, you lost the right to manage.

I am staggered, when there is so much criticism of private landlords, that this scheme was not rolled out by other local authorities or central government. It radically improved the condition and management of the private housing stock in Salford. There is always a need for social housing in the private and public sector. It needs the political will to do this. In Salford, the scheme tackled one ward at a time over several years. The Conservative governments approach appears to me, to tax the private landlord out of business. If private individuals are prepared to invest their own money in this business, it results in more social houses.

Days in the Sun

It is inevitable that this book is mainly about my career. There is next to nothing about my married life and my son Lawrence. I am very fortunate that I still love my wife of 52 years and proud of my bachelor son.

Kate and I had a childhood were there was little money for expensive holidays. I did go on holidays to Walney Island to see relatives and was so lucky that my uncle Harold (who had been my father's brother and best man) with his wife, my Auntie Maggie, made my mother and I so welcome, on all my school holidays and until she died. I also was lucky that my cousin Malcolm, Harold's son was about the same age as me. All Malcolm's friends became my friends.

During the recession years Harold went from the dole queue to walking on the wing of an aircraft. He was a stunt man for Sir Alan Cobham's flying circus, between 1928 and 1934. He with other Walney men, were out of work at the time and camping at Earnse Bay, when Cobham's circus came to Barrow.

Harold was asked if he wanted to help to sell some photographs whilst the pilot took children up in the giant moth aircraft for rides. When the circus moved on Harold was asked to join them. Harold progressed and would walk on the wing of the plane and do several stunts for the fascination of the crowd.

The plane would travel out over the sea and when it returned Harold had been replaced by a dummy. The dummy fell off over the crowd. Harold's obituary was in the Barrow paper, which went into more detail about his exploits.

Harold organised commando courses in the sand hills in north Walney. Five of us would go on bicycles, as far as possible, then walk up to the point, where the hills were higher. When the tide was out, it would leave gullies with up to 6 ft of water in them.

We had to walk flat footed along the gulley to trap fluke fish under our feet. He would take us up to the top of the hills and we would jump off to climb many more hills. The problem was that between the sand, there was small thorns growing which, for several days after, we were extracting from the soles of our feet. We also had many camping nights, up in the sand hills and at Earnse Bay, near the 5-mile beach.

Malcolm also played rugby league for Walney Central and represented the county and Great Britain in the amateur game, playing centre 3 quarter.

Kate and I made up for lack of holidays in our youth and have travelled extensively since.

After I retired, it was possible to go away for longer periods. We planned a holiday to go to New Zealand for 2 months and Kate's brother, Anthony, was able to give good advice and still does. He and his girlfriend had given up their jobs and sold their houses to travel all over the world, on long walking trips.

He married Susan Mitchell, an ideal partner, she could carry a rucksack, nearly as heavy he could, and wanted to see the world as much as he did.

We went to South Africa, and we were able to visit Mike

Smith. We met his family, and he took us in his pick-up truck to 3 safari parks.

We have also had holidays in Australia, South Africa, Thailand, Laos, Cambodia, Vietnam, China, North America and Canada, as well as many visits to Europe and the Balkan countries.

We have been fortunate and have been able to send Lawrence to Stonyhurst College, near Clitheroe, for 2 years before university. Lawrence went to St Anselm's in Birkenhead up to O-level and he was in the same class as Austin Healey. Unfortunately, from my point of view, he was not keen on rugby and preferred football. I went to watch Stonyhurst play St Anselm's in a rugby match, and Stonyhurst were hammered.

Lawrence is a now a freelance graphic designer based in London.

Lawrence aged 50

Retirement

Following retirement in 2004, I increased my fitness level to be able to walk twice a week for over 15 miles. In the early years with the club, I did all the walks in the different categories A, B and C. The walks I preferred were the B walks, averaging 10 miles, usually with the best scenery and exploring more parts of the UK.

The A walks were more limited to where there are mountains, and it was going up all morning and descending all afternoon. Also, in winter with darkness about 4pm it was not possible to complete any of the best A walks. In my late 70s, I lost confidence in my balance when exposed on high ground, so I then only did the B and C walks.

- A. Mountain walk, usually with more than 600 m (2000 ft) of ascent
- B. Moorland walks, usually with more than 300 m (1000 ft.) of ascent
- C. Mainly pastoral walk usually with less than 300 m (1000 ft) of ascent

Members' participation in any walk is subject to the discretion of the leader.

The club had 2 weekends away each year in March and October and several day coach trips to distance locations.

Myself and eight of my friends, formed a splinter group to do some of the long-distance walks in England. We were away for a week in early July and did the Donnington Brewery Walk around the Cotswolds, the North Devon Coastal Walk, St Oswald's walk from Holy Island, past Bamburgh Castle going south, the Jurassic Coastal walk in Dorset and a walk around the Isle of Man. We walked up to 15 miles per day and drank a few pints each evening. We had hot weather on each trip. The first trip in the Cotswolds, two SAS soldiers died of the heat on an exercise. We did get blisters, but we all had a great time.

I enjoyed my walking and leading on many walks over the years, until 2019. I had led a walk around the Llantysilio, a range of hills, on the far side of Llangollen for over 15 years. It was a challenging walk. In summer, it had gravel and loose stones on each of the 3 steep descents.

I thought it was better to do the walk in January as the ground would be wet, if not frozen. On this occasion, the first Sunday in January, I was wheezing all day, nobody noticed, but I knew I had a health problem. After two biopsies, I was diagnosed with cancer, non-Hodgkin's lymphoma, cancer of the lymphatic system.

This system is part of the body's immune system. I was advised by a senior nurse that this cancer, although it had reached stage 3 and many lymph nodes were swollen (infected), it may or may not be what kills you. What is more likely to kill you is getting an infection, so no pubs, no meals out, no travel on public transport etc.

I had watched and nursed my mother, for 12 months, before

she died of cancer, so I knew what to expect. Although the 18 weeks of chemotherapy was an awful experience, I remembered that my mother's experience had been worse. I had the usual side effects of being nauseated but not the retching and losing my hair.

The treatment started on 9 May 2019 and by the end of August I was in remission. The cancer has not come back. Nevertheless, it did leave me with a weak immune system. I have had many age-related problems since. The most recent being a prostate operation (no cancer involved) but a very unpleasant holmium laser enucleation of the prostate (HoLEP). It took me several months to recover. I am so fortunate to have had my cancer treatment in 2019 and not recently.

In recent years, I have been making contact with old colleagues and thanking them for the happy times we had working together. The most important being Ken Linfoot, who had persuaded me to stick at the correspondence course and gave me the basic confidence to challenge life.

Ken had done incredibly well after leaving Rushtons, working for Manchester City Estates, deputy at Reddish development corporation, Birmingham City Council, a private firm of developers and then setting up his own firm of house builders, Linfoot Country Homes. I had tracked him down on the internet and telephoned him.

He was delighted to hear from me and insisted that my wife and I had a weekend with him and Helen. We went on the Friday and spent most of first day visiting his completed small up-market residential developments. He asked me to spot the social housing on each estate and I could not. He had won lots of awards for the quality of his developments.

Ken's logic was, that if you build to high standards, residents

will respect and maintain at the same level. I asked Ken why did Fred Abbott employ me? Ken said he thought Leigh people were the salt of the earth. The Linfoots were lavish in their entertainment. I did visit him 6 months later. His cancer had returned, and it was not long after, that Kate and I went to his funeral.

Some may say there are many pearls of wisdom in this book, but is there any, I would pass on to those now considering what they should do as a career. The obvious ones are get paid for doing something you enjoy, be ambitious and remember that fortune favours the brave.

I think I may have bored you, the reader to death, so I am grateful

Kate, Lawrence and I

you have finished the book. You will be the judge of whether growing up in Leigh, was as beneficial, as I do. Alternatively, you may consider that it was a question of putting "mind over matter" in all of life's important decisions!

In my opinion the culture that existed in Leigh and Wigan when I was growing up started to die with the closure of the last cotton mill and coal mine. For some inexplicable reason I think it was a privilege to have lived in Leigh at that time.

Nevertheless, what happened in cotton and coal was not unique in British industry. Over my life time, the world has become a lot more competitive and if industry and commerce do not remain at the forefront of the latest technology, they will not survive. This is obvious in ship-building, the submarine industry and the aircraft industry. Many of the trades that were important when I left school are no longer relevant. If you visit airbus in North

Wales, you will find a modern factory that provides a perfect example.

The fact is that cotton and coal was no longer competitive. In any negotiations for reform, Luddite thinking should not exist.

Appendix

I have been very fortunate to have had some excellent colleagues throughout my career, some a lot brighter than I am. I have been able to learn from their experience. I thank you all from the bottom of my heart. Nevertheless, what we have been able to achieve is modest compared to the giants in the property business.

I have been able to observe, from near and afar, some of these great men. I will be bold and provide my own Hall of Fame, who I would take my hat off to. I think John Whittaker's purchase of the Manchester Ship Canal Company was a stroke of genius and he can't be equalled in capitalising on all the opportunities presented.

Close behind is Trevor Hemmings, who my friend Gerry Hamilton worked for twice. Next John Hall, developer of the Metro centre in Gateshead, a good friend to Malcolm Clarke. Next Kevin McCabe of Kevin McCabe group international, who came on board with my team, to advise on developing the Co-op headquarters in Morrison Street, Glasgow, a magnificent building seen as you travel over the Kingston Bridge, on the M8 as you leave Glasgow. It took some time for Glasgow City Council to give planning consent. Nevertheless, we could not secure an anchor tenant. I think this was a matter of timing. John Lewis had plans to invest in the north but in an ordered way.

It was several years later that Cheadle Royal Business Park was developed, a similar site. Last, I will include my friend Gerry Hamilton, with his silver trowel, who rose from laying bricks to many directorships. Bless your cotton socks, Gerry, that your mother turned down so they would be easy to put on in the morning!

If you have reached the grand old age of eighty and can brag with the best, I would be obliged if you can consider the poem by Saxon White Kessinger "The Indispensable Man." This poem does not apply to women!